IN THE
KITCHEN
WITH
*Michael Salmon*

RECIPES OF DISTINCTION FROM THE *Hartstone Inn*

Bonnie & John,

Flavor a recipe with love and it will delight any palate. Happy Cooking!

March 2014

Michael Salmon

CHEF MICHAEL SALMON

# IN THE KITCHEN WITH
# Michael Salmon

RECIPES OF DISTINCTION FROM THE *Hartstone Inn*

MICHAEL SALMON

PHOTOGRAPHER: HAL HAGY

CONTRIBUTING WRITER: ELIZABETH ILGENFRITZ

Inquiries should be addressed to:
Michael Salmon
Hartstone Inn
41 Elm Street
Camden, Maine 04843
www.hartstoneinn.com

Author: Michael Salmon

Library of Congress Control Number: 2006907689

ISBN: 0-9729919-1-3

Photographs by: Hal Hagy, Lucky Dog Gallery, Rockport, Maine

Illustrations by: Judy Sullivan

Designed by: Harrah Lord, Yellow House Studio, Rockport, Maine

Edited by: Elizabeth IlgenFritz, South Montville, Maine

Printed by: P. Chan & Edward, Inc.

Printed in China

FIRST EDITION

# Contents

# ACKNOWLEDGMENT

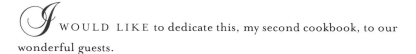

*I* WOULD LIKE to dedicate this, my second cookbook, to our wonderful guests.

My first cookbook was a great success, and I would like to thank all of our devoted guests who have offered so much encouragement and support over the years. When we took over the Inn in 1998, we had big dreams and aspirations for the Inn and our business. Since then, each room in the Inn has been transformed (some several times) to reach our standards, and the property is finally feeling like it has evolved into the Inn of our dreams. Our repeat guests are a large part of our success, and Mary Jo, the staff and I look forward to greeting familiar faces each and every day. There are nights in the dining room when I feel as if I am throwing a large dinner party for a group of friends! I wish I could name all of you here and thank you personally in this book, but my editor would kill me. So once again, a big thank you to each and every one of you. We look forward to many visits in the years to come.

Innkeeping itself is a very time-consuming occupation. Add to it dinner service, cooking classes and renovations at the Inn, and very little time is left for anything else, much less the writing of a second cookbook. So I would like to once again, thank my wife Mary Jo for her dedication and understanding over the past few years. How many couples do you know who could work side by side each and every day from the first pot of coffee in the morning until the last table is reset after dinner each night? For all of you who have been fortunate enough to get to know Mary Jo, you know how very special she is. Take normal love, multiply it by a million and add a few more, and you reach the level of my love for her.

Several very talented people have collaborated with me on this book and I would like to thank them for their dedication and hard work. Elizabeth IlgenFritz was the editor of my first cookbook and agreed to return to battle for the second time around. I am not quite sure how I talked her into it, but I was fortunate enough to get Elizabeth to do some writing for me in addition to the editing of this cookbook. I sent her out on individual assignments to collect information and write about area activities from winter tobogganing to lobstering. She was a real trooper (I told her I wouldn't mention the seasickness thing — she claims it was the 2,000 pounds of dead bait!) and she was able to capture the essence of each story as I had hoped, adding a bit of wit and interest to each subject. Thank you, Elizabeth! Another alumnus of the first book is Harrah Lord. Harrah is responsible for the design of the book. Just as she did in the first cookbook, Harrah takes all of the individual pieces of work, my recipes, Hal's photographs, Elizabeth's essays, Joe's wine notes, Judy's illustrations, and weaves them together to create the finished project. As before, she has done a wonderful job and I am grateful for her tireless efforts. A new twist for this book is the matching of each food item with a specific wine type. For expert advice, I turned to a good friend Joe Nardone. Joe has been in the wine business for a very long time (in the Boston area) and has always impressed me with his wealth of wine knowledge and his ability to match a wine perfectly with the dish at hand. Judy Sullivan is a school administrator down near Dallas, Texas, and has been to the Inn several times. Mutual friends of ours introduced us to some of Judy's beautiful artwork from her recent trips to Maine, and I knew they would be perfect for my cookbook, and they are. She agreed to have them included, and I am very grateful to her. The final piece of the puzzle was the photographer. I met Hal Hagy at the Camden "Harbor Arts" fair last year and was taken by his talent as a photographer. Not only does he have an instinctive eye for capturing those special moments in time, Hal is also one of the nicest guys you'll ever meet. It was a real pleasure working with him, and if normal photographs are worth a thousand words, his are worth a million.

Mary Jo and I are very involved with the day-to-day operation of the Inn, but we can't be there every moment of every day. Our staff is a vital part of our success and I would like them to know how much I appreciate them and their diligent efforts to keep the Inn running smoothly. Our superstar housekeeper Georgia (from Jamaica) has been with us five years and I look forward to her arrival each spring and dread her departure each fall. She's not real big on the snow thing. Holly is our right hand at the Inn and she oversees the day-to-day operation when we are not there. What a joy it is working with you, Holly. Karen, our assistant innkeeper, has been with us part-time for two years now and is always cheerful and fun to work with. Thank you.

I kid around that I have a "Midwest distributor" for my cookbook. Mary Jo's grandfather, Cecil Brink, sells a copy of my book to nearly everyone he meets. Thank you, Grandpa, for all of your efforts in promoting the Inn and my cookbook. Oh, by the way, I have a few cases of this new cookbook coming your way.

# $\mathcal{I}$NTRODUCTION

$\mathcal{O}$NE OF THE EXCITING PARTS of my job is the opportunity I have to explore new dishes and recipes at the Inn, without being locked into a defined cuisine or style. This allows me to grow as a cook and experiment with new ingredients and techniques. The by-product of this, however, is the frequent Inn or dinner guest who asks, "Is this recipe in the cookbook?" to which I reply, "No, but I promise it will be in the next one." After a few years of compiling and testing recipes (I am much more experienced the second time around), the time has come to fulfill that promise. The cooking classes I offer throughout the year give me the chance to refine the recipes and force me to sit down and turn my thoughts and creations into written form. I love my work at the Inn and take great pleasure in transforming those experiences into a cookbook for all of you to enjoy.

With a second book comes the anxiety of living up to certain expectations created by the success of the first cookbook. After developing a set of recipes, based on our activities at the Inn, I chose to form the foundation of the book in a similar pattern to that of the first cookbook. Recipes are classified into specific sections, starting with breakfast and ending with the various ethnic cuisines offered in our cooking classes. I have included a special section on Julia Child in the beginning of the book that includes a dedication to her and recipes I prepared for her on her trip to the Inn in August 2001. Throughout the book you will also find essays written by Elizabeth IlgenFritz that highlight some of Mary Jo's and my favorite experiences in the Camden area — from sailing on Penobscot Bay aboard the historical schooner *Surprise* to gliding down a chute of ice on a toboggan at the Camden Snow Bowl.

Mary Jo's enthusiasm for growing and displaying orchids continues at the Inn. She

always has orchids in bloom, arranging them throughout the common rooms of the Inn for our guests to enjoy. Elizabeth interviewed Mary Jo for an essay about orchids, touching briefly on their history and including some notes on orchid cultivation, accompanied by some of Hal Hagy's amazing orchid photographs.

Guests to Maine are captivated by our lobsters, as they should be. For most, lobsters are a real treat and recollections of a lobster feast at one of the many lobster pounds in the area will linger in their memories for years to come. Most guests, however, miss out on a very magical part of the lobster cycle, lobster fishing. The *Lively Lady Too* is a local boat that leaves Camden Harbor each day taking guests on an "Eco Tour," which demystifies the process of catching lobsters. For those who miss out on the adventure, I have set aside a section in this book featuring my favorite Maine lobsterman, Bert Witham.

Bert's family has been lobstering in Maine for generations and I was fortunate enough to join him one morning (very early) aboard his vessel *Lobstar* to see him in action. The stories that man can tell!

My passion for food is followed closely by my love for wine. A good friend of mine, Joe Nardone, is an expert on wine and has the ability and knowledge to match wine with food in an uncanny manner. Wine speak, as I call it, is the terminology that wine experts use to define the qualities of a wine. Sometimes I get it, and other times I don't. Joe has a way of defining the qualities of each wine and the ability to explain, in plain terms, why those qualities will match with particular foods. He has written an essay on the subject, and you will also find Joe's wine pairing notes in the sidebars next to each appropriate recipe, where an education in wine awaits you.

Mary Jo and I enjoy mixing cocktails, experimenting with different recipes and ingredients and creating our own concoctions. We feature some of these drink specials each evening at the Inn (some have become regulars) and get quite a few requests from our guests for cocktail recipes. I have included a small section on our favorite cocktails and drinks, showcasing some of these unique and flavorful libations. Get your shaker out.

The section on spices and spice blends highlights some of my favorite combinations of herbs and spices and their uses. Having a ready-mixed spice blend on hand can make things so much easier in the kitchen and can transform a regular dish into something extraordinary. Recipes for my spice blends are found throughout both of my cookbooks and are referenced by page number in this section on spices.

One of my other culinary passions is the collecting of antique chocolate molds. I have been collecting them since my early twenties (not that long ago!) and I have them displayed on the walls and shelves of my kitchens. Some of my favorite molds appear throughout the cookbook. You will find even more in the section on chocolate molds, where I have included some instructions on using these antique works of art.

It is such a joy seeing a book come together, from the initial conception to the first printed copy. I hope you enjoy reading and preparing the recipes as much as I have enjoyed putting this cookbook together. May your travels bring you back to Camden and the Hartstone Inn soon, and if you haven't been our way, please stop by.

Happy Cooking!
Michael Salmon

# A Love for Orchids

IN MICHAEL AND MARY JO'S NINTH YEAR, as their business continues to expand and diversify so does Mary Jo's collection of orchids, which have grown to 450 plants. Now that they have additional staff, Mary Jo has had more time to learn about her orchids and her greenhouse. After losing a few orchids over the winter, she realized those particular plants need to dry out more during the colder months. Mary Jo kept an eye on another orchid in her greenhouse and watched as it flourished under cover of a bushier orchid on a shelf above. The leaves of the bushier orchid had created a cooler, shadier growing area beneath it. Through trial and error, Mary Jo is delighted that she's been able to create four growing subclimates in her greenhouse.

Orchids have been around for centuries, but it wasn't until the early 1800s that they became a household name — in Britain, anyway. For safekeeping, when a British explorer William Swanson shipped some tropical plants from Brazil to England, he used other tropical plants (orchids) because of their thick stems and masses of leaves as packing material. Fortunately, a man named Cattley received some of Swanson's shipment, and for whatever reason, put some of the "packing material" in his greenhouse. When they flowered that winter, he fell in love with this particular pink flowering orchid. Soon, many other Europeans did as well. This pink beauty (Cattleya libiata) caused almost everyone in Britain's high society to want one. (Mary Jo also loves them for their large, frilly corsage blossoms and the fragrance that many varieties offer. "They can make an entire room smell absolutely wonderful.")

So desperate were the wealthy for orchids that some men became professional orchid hunters, and if they survived the hunt and the competition and made it back to Europe from the tropics, they often became wealthy themselves, and honored. Each orchid variety was often named after its discoverer. Most of these amazing plants were auctioned off in London to the highest bidder, and excessive amounts of money were spent for the privilege of owning these prized beauties. Soon, experimentation with orchids began. Varieties were cultivated, hybrids appeared,

and eventually, propagation from seed transpired. Finally, everyone interested in orchids could afford to own some of these alluring plants.

Mary Jo loves that you can buy affordable orchids. She recommends picking one up at Home Depot or your local grocery store for as little as twenty dollars. If you kill it, it will have already lasted two to three months, which is much longer than cut flowers do. As your interests grow and you want to acquire more specialized orchids, Mary Jo highly recommends buying from these three fabulous growers: Carmelaorchids.net, Kalapanatropicals.net and Carterandholmes.com.

Not unlike other orchid enthusiasts, Mary Jo's interest in orchids has only continued to develop. Once settled in the Northeast after leaving the Caribbean, she began to buy orchids, one or two at a time, until she'd amassed fifty in a single year. She started out with varieties known to be easy to grow, but it wasn't

long before Mary Jo was experimenting with rare varieties as well. Being adventurous, she learned a lot about these tantalizing creatures primarily through trial and error, a little luck at times and persistence. Her expertise clearly shows now in each and every one of her healthy, flowering orchids.

Her 450 plants provide rotation so that blooming orchids can be in the Inn's common areas year-round. Mary Jo has a great eye for color and texture, and her various and vibrant collection allows her to create winning combinations with stunning effect. When they're not at the Inn, the orchids reside in the custom greenhouse that Michael had built for her, complete with humidity system, water storage tanks and an automatic heat and ventilation system. Some of Mary Jo's favorite orchids, Vandas and Ascocendas, don't do well in the Inn. They grow best in a controlled environment while suspended in bamboo baskets, their dangling roots exposed, so these vibrant tangerine or lavender blossomed orchids hang from the ceiling in the greenhouse for her to enjoy while she's working there.

Mary Jo will be the first to tell you that if you want to cultivate orchids, you need to be willing to experiment and to be prepared to lose some. You should have a place in mind where you intend to place your orchids because some varieties like to sit near a sunny window while others

prefer indirect light. Mary Jo says the best advice for someone who wants to start growing orchids is to really look at your environment and see what conditions you will be able to offer. What kind of humidity does your home have? How much light exists in your rooms?

Phalaenopsis (phals), Paphiopedilum (paphs) and Oncidiums (onc) are varieties that Mary Jo finds most easy to grow in the home. These hybrids are usually considered "beginner orchids," largely because they will re-bloom under the conditions that most windowsill growers can offer. They require less light, about the same as for African violets, and will adapt to the humidity levels that are present in most homes.

Orchids can be grown on a tray of pebbles with water, which prevents the pots from sitting directly in the water while providing needed humidity. Orchids like to be kept warm during the day and a little cooler at night. It's true that watering orchids does seem to give those unfamiliar with growing orchids the most trouble. Mary Jo waters her orchids once a week. During the summer, they get watered every five days. Basically, the hotter the temperature, the more water they need, and the colder it is, the opposite holds true. It's all simply a matter of practice.

There is no question that Mary Jo finds cultivating orchids extremely satisfying and rewarding. The next time you're in Camden, stop in at the Hartstone Inn to see her orchids. They're worthy of a visit. ■

# A Tribute to Julia Child

### August 15, 1912 — August 13, 2004

Mastering the Art of
FRENCH COOKING

BY JULIA CHILD
LOUISETTE BERTHOLLE
SIMONE BECK

NEW YORK
Alfred · A · Knopf

1966

As a child and aspiring chef, I was captivated by the various cooking series on PBS (the ancestor of the food network) and regularly watched shows like the "Master Chefs" series, Jacques Pepin's cooking show and, of course, Julia Child's show, "The French Chef."

I used to write down recipes during the television programs and catalog them along with other recipe clippings in a binder for future use. Julia Child was always an inspiration to me with her "no nonsense" approach to French cooking. During a trip to Colorado while I was in my mid-teens, I had my first opportunity to review her cookbook, *Mastering the Art of French Cooking,* and I was intrigued. My hosts graciously invited me into their kitchen and I created my first recipe from her book — crème caramels. I had witnessed the preparation of these decadent custards at the bistro restaurant where I was working, but had never had a hand at it myself. Needless to say, they turned out great and I became a big fan of the book.

Soon after, I purchased my first copy of the book and read it cover to cover. In her recipes, I was introduced to unusual ingredients like sweetbreads, marzipan and marrow, items that were not common in rural Midwest cooking. Years later my mother gave me an early (1966) edition of the cookbook as a gift and it has become a favorite in my cookbook collection.

On August 10, 2001, we were honored with the presence of Julia Child in our dining room at the Inn. Julia was on one of her last visits to her summer home in Deer Isle, Maine, and spent the evening in Camden and had dinner with us at the Inn. It was such a pleasure to have the opportunity to prepare dinner for such an icon. Sure, over my long career of working in resort hotels I had prepared dinner for many celebrities, from Sean Connery to Barry Manilow, but this was a whole different story. Her voice was unmistakable; she was very gracious and complimentary.

Nancy Harmon Jenkins, a local food writer who accompanied Julia to dinner that evening, had briefed me on some of Julia's favorite foods — Maine lobster and lamb. The menu I ultimately decided on incorporated these two items and was influenced by both my love of various ethnic cuisines and the use of seasonal food products. Of course, I had to finish the meal with one of my famous soufflés.

During dinner, Julia asked Mary Jo if we had any children and Mary Jo replied, "Yes, we have two cats." She talked about her love of cats and asked if she could see them after dinner. While she was finishing her dessert, I got busy cleaning the kitchen. At the time, we lived directly behind the kitchen in an area that is now a guest room. When she arrived in the kitchen, I went back and retrieved our cats and she held each one, petting them and talking to them. She complimented the dinner, posed for a few pictures and graciously autographed the 1966 edition of her cookbook that my mother had given to me.

Julia influenced many of us over the years, so I would like to dedicate this section of my cookbook to her and take a moment to honor her and to express my sincere gratitude for the inspiration she gave to me.

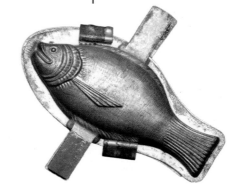

# Seared Chinese Five Spice Quail with Ginger-Tossed Vegetables

SERVES 4

4 SEMI-BONELESS QUAIL
1 TABLESPOON SESAME OIL
3 TABLESPOONS CANOLA OIL
1 TEASPOON CHINESE FIVE SPICE
2 TABLESPOONS SOY SAUCE

1 TABLESPOON KOSHER SALT
1/2 CUP FINELY JULIENNED CARROT
1/2 CUP SLICED SNOW PEAS
1/2 CUP RED BELL PEPPER JULIENNE
1/2 CUP THINLY SLICED BOK CHOY
1/2 TEASPOON FINELY MINCED FRESH GINGERROOT
2 TEASPOONS SESAME OIL
1 TABLESPOON SOY SAUCE
1/2 TEASPOON EACH BLACK AND WHITE SESAME SEEDS
1/2 CUP GINGER DRESSING (RECIPE FOLLOWS)
OPTIONAL GARNISH: DEEP-FRIED CELLOPHANE NOODLES

1. Marinate the quail in a bowl by combining it with the two oils, Chinese five spice and soy sauce. Toss to evenly coat. Marinate for 2 hours.

2. Bring 1 quart of water to a boil in a medium-sized saucepan with 1 Tablespoon of kosher salt.

3. Prepare the vegetables: Peel the carrots and remove the ends. Finely julienne the carrots either by hand or with a mandoline. I find that the plastic Oriental

Cellophane noodles make a perfect garnish for this dish. When fried in hot oil, the noodles puff, creating the appearance of a nest, maybe a quail's nest. Cellophane noodles are also known as bean threads or bean thread noodles and are made from mung bean starch and water. They are sold dried in small bundles. For this dish, heat some oil until very hot, drop in the dry noodles in small batches and remove as soon as they puff up. Drain on paper towels. ■

*While the richness of the
quail may call for a light red
wine, the spice and ginger make
an aromatic white a more
complete match. The viognier
grape with its floral and
honeysuckle aromas, hint of
sweetness and crisp acidity
bring all the flavors of the dish
into complete focus. Cline and
Kunde vineyards from Sonoma
both make excellent examples of
this varietal.* ∎

mandoline works very well when you want to achieve a fine julienne. Snap the ends off the snow peas and pull away the strings. Stack a few snow peas and cut into a fine julienne. Remove the ends from the red bell pepper and cut the pepper in half. Remove the seeds and ribs and place the pepper halves skin side down on the cutting board. Carefully slice the pepper into two thin layers by keeping the knife blade parallel to the cutting board and slowly slicing the pepper into two thin sheets, following the skin. Put the two halves back together and slice into a fine julienne.

4. When the water boils, add the carrots. Blanch for 20 seconds and add the snow peas and red bell pepper julienne. Remove immediately to an ice bath to cool. Drain the blanched vegetables and reserve until serving. At the last moment, combine the vegetables, bok choy, minced ginger, sesame oil, soy sauce and sesame seeds in a medium-sized bowl and toss.

5. Just before serving, preheat the oven to 350 degrees. Heat a grill pan over high heat. When the pan is very hot, add the quail and grill for about 2 minutes on each side. Place the quail on an ovenproof pan and finish cooking in the preheated oven for 10 minutes.

6. To serve, place a bed of the tossed vegetables on each plate. Top with the warm grilled quail and drizzle each plate with 2 Tablespoons of the ginger dressing. Garnish with deep-fried cellophane noodles if desired.

## GINGER DRESSING

MAKES 1 1/2 CUPS

1/2 CUP RICE WINE VINEGAR
1/4 CUP SOY SAUCE
1 1/2 TABLESPOONS HOISIN SAUCE
1 TEASPOON DRY MUSTARD POWDER
1 TEASPOON GRANULATED SUGAR

1 TABLESPOON MINCED GINGER
1 TABLESPOON MINCED SHALLOTS
1/2 TEASPOON MINCED GARLIC
2 TABLESPOONS SESAME OIL
1/3 CUP CANOLA OIL

1. Combine all the ingredients, except for the oils, in a blender. Blend for 30 seconds to combine well.

2. With the blender still running, drizzle in the two oils and blend for an additional 10 seconds.

# MIXED BABY GREENS WITH A PAPAYA SEED DRESSING AND MAINE LOBSTER

SERVES 4

TWO 1 1/4 POUND LIVE MAINE LOBSTERS
1 LARGE VINE-RIPENED TOMATO
1 HAAS AVOCADO
6 OUNCES MIXED BABY GREENS
PAPAYA SEED DRESSING (RECIPE FOLLOWS)
1/2 CUP CRISP HOMEMADE CROUTONS

1. Fill a large 9-quart stockpot with two inches of water; cover and bring to a boil. Add live lobsters, cover and cook for 10 minutes. Remove from the water and let cool. When cool, crack lobsters and remove the meat from the claws, knuckles and tails (discarding the vein). Cut the tail fin in half (resulting in four 1/2 tail fins) and reserve for garnish. Discard the remaining shells.

2. Slice the lobster tails in half lengthwise and reserve with the tail fins.

3. Core and slice the tomato into 8 equal wedges. Cut the avocado in half,

*I serve a crusty country-style bread in the restaurant for dinner and use this bread to make the croutons, which are sprinkled on our salads and soups. Cut the bread into 1/2-inch cubes and place in a hot sauté pan set over medium heat. Drizzle the cubed bread with extra virgin olive oil (1 Tablespoon olive oil for every cup of cubed bread) and stir every couple of minutes until uniformly brown and crisp. Season with kosher salt, cool and store in an airtight container until needed.* ■

remove the pit and use a melon baller to remove uniformly round balls of the avocado flesh.

4. To serve, toss the greens with enough of the papaya seed dressing to coat well. Place a bed of the greens on four chilled salad plates and top each mound of greens with a quarter of the lobster meat. Surround the salads with two tomato wedges and equally distribute the avocado balls between the plates. Drizzle the lobster with a little of the papaya seed dressing. Sprinkle each salad with the crisp croutons and garnish with the ½ tail fin. Serve.

### PAPAYA SEED DRESSING

1/2 CUP RICE WINE VINEGAR
1/2 CUP GRANULATED SUGAR
1/2 CUP CANOLA OIL
1/4 CUP CHOPPED VIDALIA ONION
1/2 CUP CHOPPED FRESH PAPAYA
1 TABLESPOON PAPAYA SEEDS
1/2 TEASPOON KOSHER SALT
1/2 TEASPOON DRY MUSTARD

1. Combine all the ingredients above in a blender and blend until smooth.

2. Refrigerate until needed. *Will keep for up to 2 weeks.*

# PEACH SORBET

SERVES 10

1 CUP GRANULATED SUGAR
1/4 CUP LEMON JUICE
1 POUND FRESH OR FROZEN PEACHES
    (REMOVE SKINS, SEEDS AND PITS)
1/4 CUP LIGHT CORN SYRUP

## Wine Notes

*Chardonnay is the classical match for almost any lobster dish, but it is the preparation and accompanying sides and sauces that help to pick the right one. In this case, the tropical papaya calls for a lighter un-oaked version of the grape. A good Macon-Villages will display the necessary citrus and tropical fruit while still maintaining good acidity to cut through the richness of the lobster. Domaine Comte Lafon is one of the best producers. ■*

1. Make a simple syrup: Combine 1 cup of water and the sugar in a 4-quart saucepan and bring to a boil, giving it a gentle stir every 30 seconds. Once the boil is reached, reduce the heat to low and simmer for 5 minutes. Remove from the heat and cool.

2. Place the lemon juice and peaches in a food processor or blender, and puree until very smooth, about 2 minutes. Combine the peach puree, the cooled simple syrup and the corn syrup in a bowl and refrigerate for 2 hours to cool.

3. Prepare your ice cream maker for freezing, and follow the manufacturer's instructions for making sorbet/ice cream.

# Hazelnut-Encrusted Rack of Lamb with a Merlot Bordelaise and Chive Smashed Potatoes

SERVES 4

4 FULL RACKS OF NEW ZEALAND LAMB, FRENCHED
KOSHER SALT AND FRESHLY GROUND BLACK PEPPER
3 TABLESPOONS EXTRA VIRGIN OLIVE OIL
4 TABLESPOONS DIJON MUSTARD
1/2 CUP PANKO BREAD CRUMBS
2 TABLESPOONS CHOPPED FLAT LEAF PARSLEY
1/4 CUP COARSELY CHOPPED HAZELNUTS
MERLOT BORDELAISE (RECIPE FOLLOWS)
CHIVE SMASHED POTATOES (RECIPE FOLLOWS)

1. Preheat the oven to 350 degrees.

2. Heat a large sauté pan over high heat. Cut each lamb rack in half, cutting between the bones. Season the lamb racks with salt and pepper. Add

*There is an art to the making of stocks and sauces and it is a time-consuming process. If you don't have the time to make your own bordelaise from scratch, I have a wonderful bordelaise base available for sale on my website, which allows your sauce to be completed in minutes. The papaya seed dressing on the facing page is one of my favorite recipes and uses the seeds from a fresh papaya, which are quite peppery in flavor. ∎*

2 Tablespoons of the olive oil to the hot pan and sear the lamb on each side for 3 minutes.

3. Remove the lamb from the pan and place on a foil-lined baking sheet with the meat side up. Spread a Tablespoon of the Dijon mustard on each lamb rack, coating the meat evenly. Mix the bread crumbs and the parsley together and sprinkle over the mustard. Sprinkle the chopped hazelnuts over the bread crumbs and lightly press on the mixture to adhere it to the mustard.

4. Drizzle the top of the lamb racks with the remaining Tablespoon of olive oil and finish in the preheated oven for about 10 minutes (depending on the size of the lamb) for medium, or longer, if desired.

5. Serve with Chive Smashed Potatoes, Merlot Bordelaise and vegetables of your choice.

## MERLOT BORDELAISE

MAKES 2 1/2 CUPS

3 TABLESPOONS UNSALTED BUTTER
1 SHALLOT, MINCED
3 TABLESPOONS ALL-PURPOSE FLOUR
1 CUP MERLOT WINE
1/2 SMALL BAY LEAF
1 SPRIG FRESH THYME
10 BLACK PEPPERCORNS, CRACKED
2 CUPS BROWN VEAL STOCK/BROTH (HOMEMADE OR STORE BOUGHT)
KOSHER SALT TO TASTE

## Wine Notes

*As Julia would tell you, great lamb calls for great Bordeaux. In this case, the hazelnut crust demands the earthier style from either Pomerol or St. Emilion. These merlot-based appellations show deep blackberry and currant fruit with hints of warm earth and mushrooms. Chateau Lyonnat, Lussac St. Emilion or Chateau Sergant, Lalande de Pomerol are excellent and affordable choices. ■*

1. Heat a 2-quart saucepan over medium heat. Add the butter to the pan and then the minced shallot. Stir for 1 minute and add the flour. Cook, stirring for 2 minutes.

2. Add the red wine, bay leaf, thyme, peppercorns and veal stock/broth and bring to a boil. Reduce the heat to low and simmer for 15 minutes.

3. Season to taste with salt, then strain through a fine mesh strainer. *Bordelaise will keep for 1 week covered in the refrigerator and freezes well for up to 3 months.*

## CHIVE SMASHED POTATOES

> 2 POUNDS LARGE RED POTATOES
> 1 TEASPOON KOSHER SALT
> 3/4 CUP WHOLE MILK
> 1/4 CUP UNSALTED BUTTER
> 2 PINCHES WHITE PEPPER
> 2 TABLESPOONS CHOPPED CHIVES
> KOSHER SALT TO TASTE

1. Peel and cut the potatoes into ½-inch pieces. Place the potatoes in a 2-quart saucepan and cover with cold water by 1 inch and add the salt. Cover and bring to a boil over high heat. Reduce to a simmer and cook for 30 minutes.

2. Drain off all the water and add the milk, butter and white pepper. Return the potatoes to the heat for 5 minutes to warm the milk. Remove from the heat and smash the potatoes, leaving them somewhat chunky. Add the chopped chives and adjust the seasoning with salt. Can be kept covered for up to 30 minutes in a warm place before serving.

# Fresh Berry Soufflé with a Chambord Crème Anglaise

SERVES 4

1 CUP WHOLE MILK
4 TABLESPOONS UNSALTED BUTTER
1/2 CUP ALL-PURPOSE FLOUR
1/2 CUP GRANULATED SUGAR
5 LARGE EGGS, SEPARATED
1 TABLESPOON UNSALTED BUTTER, SOFT
2 TABLESPOONS GRANULATED SUGAR
1/2 CUP FRESH BERRIES (RASPBERRIES, BLACKBERRIES AND SLICED
    STRAWBERRIES)
2 TABLESPOONS CHAMBORD (RASPBERRY LIQUEUR)
1/4 TEASPOON CREAM OF TARTAR
CHAMBORD CRÈME ANGLAISE (RECIPE FOLLOWS)

1. Heat the milk, over medium heat, in a 2-quart saucepan. In another 2-quart saucepan, melt the butter over medium heat. When the butter is melted, stir in the flour and mix until combined well. Reduce heat to low, and stir frequently.

2. When the milk comes to a simmer, stir in the sugar. Continue to stir, dissolving the sugar for 2 minutes. Pour the milk mixture into the butter mixture and stir with a whisk to combine, cooking over medium heat until a ball forms and the mixture releases from the sides of the pan.

3. Immediately place the mixture in a mixing bowl and stir (using the flat paddle) on medium-low speed with an electric mixer for 10 minutes.

4. One by one, stir in the egg yolks, allowing each to be completely incorporated before adding the next. When all of the egg yolks are incorporated, set the mixture (soufflé base) aside and allow it to cool. *This base will keep refrigerated for up to 1 week.*

*I use Crème Anglaise at breakfast with pastry starters or sweet entrées like French toast or fruit-filled crepes, and for dessert at dinner, especially with our famous soufflés. Flavor it to coordinate with any dish by adding nuts, liqueurs, chocolate or spices. Crème Anglaise is also a great base for ice cream. Simply pour the flavored Crème Anglaise into a prepared ice cream maker and you can create your favorite ice creams.* ■

Wine Notes

*While most great wines are made from grapes, a few come from other fruits. Randall Graham of Bonny Doon Vineyards makes one such wine from pressed and fermented raspberries. The bright, fresh fruit and pleasant sweetness of his framboise will match wonderfully with both the flavors and texture of this soufflé.* ■

5. Generously butter four 1½ cup soufflé dishes, covering the entire surface area on the inside of the cups, including the rim. Coat the buttered cups with granulated sugar, rotating the cups to coat them evenly. Tap out any excess sugar. Set the prepared cups aside.

6. Place the soufflé base in a mixing bowl and stir in half the berries with the Chambord, mixing well.

7. Preheat the oven to 350 degrees.

8. In an electric mixer fitted with a whisk, whip the egg whites and cream of tartar to stiff peaks. With a large rubber spatula, gently fold half of the egg whites into the base. Continue folding in the remaining egg whites. Gently pour the batter into the prepared soufflé dishes, filling them ⅘ of the way full. *Be careful not to drip the batter on the rims, or the soufflés may not rise evenly.*

9. Bake in the center of a 350-degree oven for 35 minutes, or until lightly browned on top. Remove from the oven, place on a small serving plate and top with a small mound of the reserved fresh berries. Dust with powdered sugar and hurry the soufflés to the table. Serve the soufflés with a side of Chambord Crème Anglaise, pouring the crème Anglaise into a hole you poke in the top of the soufflé at the table. Eat immediately.

## CRÈME ANGLAISE

> 2 CUPS WHOLE MILK
> 3 LARGE EGGS
> 2 EGG YOLKS
> ½ CUP GRANULATED SUGAR

1. Select the desired flavor from the list that follows, making the required changes as noted.

2. Heat the milk in a 2-quart saucepan over medium-high heat and bring to a simmer.

3. In a medium-sized mixing bowl, whisk together the eggs, egg yolks and sugar. Have ready a large bowl half full of ice water (with plenty of ice) and a medium-sized bowl that will fit inside the ice bath. Also have a fine mesh strainer, a wooden spoon and an instant read thermometer.

4. When the milk reaches a simmer, slowly pour about ½ cup of the hot milk into the egg mixture, whisking constantly. This is called tempering. Add another ½ cup of hot milk, whisking constantly. Now whisk the tempered egg mixture back into the saucepan with the milk, whisking constantly. Set the whisk aside and stir this mixture with the wooden spoon constantly over medium heat until the mixture reaches a temperature of 175 degrees on the instant read thermometer or until the mixture just coats the back of the spoon. Remove from the heat and immediately pour the mixture through the fine mesh strainer into the medium bowl. Immediately set this bowl in the ice bath to stop the cooking. Stir the mixture, occasionally, until it cools. *Refrigerate in a covered container until needed, for up to 1 week.*

VANILLA: Steep the milk with ½ a fresh vanilla bean, scraping out the seeds (or add 1 teaspoon of vanilla extract to the finished sauce)

GINGER: Steep the milk with 1 teaspoon freshly grated ginger

CHAMBORD: Add ½ cup fresh raspberries and 1 Tablespoon Chambord after it cools

CHOCOLATE: Stir in ¼ cup chocolate syrup

ALMOND: Add 2 teaspoons crushed toasted almonds with 1 Tablespoon Amaretto

HAZELNUT: Add 2 teaspoons crushed hazelnuts with 1 Tablespoon Frangelico

Breakfast
at the Inn

# BREAKFAST JUICES

At the Inn, we serve a
variety of different
blended juices. The key
to any good juice is the
fruit you begin with.
Frozen fruit works well
in these drinks if the
particular fruit you are
looking for is out of
season or just not ripe.
Experiment with various
fruits and juices . . .
we do!

*When using frozen berries for juices, look for IQF (Individually Quick Frozen) berries without added sugar. This will get you the closest to fresh berry flavor. In addition to the fresh fruits and juices, other ingredients can be added to create unique flavor combinations. Coconut cream such as "Coco-Lopez" adds a rich coconut flavor, but is also quite sweet so use sparingly. Honey or maple syrup can also be mixed in for additional sweetness, if desired. ▪*

## MANGO AND RASPBERRY JUICE

SERVES 4

1 RIPE MANGO
1 CUP FRESH OR FROZEN RASPBERRIES
3 CUPS FRESHLY SQUEEZED ORANGE JUICE

1. Peel and seed the mango. Cut into 1-inch pieces and place in a blender with the raspberries and orange juice.

2. Blend at medium speed for 1 minute or until well blended. Serve chilled.

## TROPICAL FRUIT SMOOTHIE

SERVES 4

2 CUPS RIPE TROPICAL FRUIT (PAPAYA, MANGO, KIWI, BANANA, PINEAPPLE, GUAVA, CARAMBOLA, PASSION FRUIT, ETC. — USE ANY COMBINATION OF ONE OR MORE FRUITS)
1 CUP FRESHLY SQUEEZED ORANGE JUICE
1 CUP PINEAPPLE JUICE
1 CUP VANILLA YOGURT

1. Prepare the fruit.

   PAPAYA AND MANGO: Peel, seed and cut into chunks

   KIWI AND BANANA: Peel and cut into chunks

   PINEAPPLE: Peel, core and cut into chunks

GUAVA: Peel and cut into chunks, and blend with the orange juice, then strain out the seeds

CARAMBOLA: Cut into chunks, blend with the orange juice, then strain out the seeds

PASSION FRUIT: Cut in half, squeeze the juice and seeds into the orange juice, mix and strain out the seeds (use a maximum of 2 passion fruits for this recipe)

2. Place the fruit in the blender with the juices and yogurt and blend at medium speed for 1 minute, or until well blended. Serve chilled.

## STRAWBERRY AND BANANA JUICE

SERVES 4

2 RIPE BANANAS
1 CUP SLICED RIPE STRAWBERRIES
3 CUPS FRESHLY SQUEEZED ORANGE JUICE

1. Peel the bananas and remove the stems from the strawberries. Cut into 1-inch pieces and place in a blender with the orange juice.

2. Blend at medium speed for 1 minute or until well blended. Serve chilled.

# LEMON MOUSSE TRIFLE

SERVES 4

1/2 CUP HEAVY CREAM
1/2 CUP VANILLA YOGURT
1/2 CUP LEMON CURD (SEE CITRUS CURD RECIPE, PAGE 55)
1 CUP GRANOLA
2 CUPS CHOPPED FRESH FRUIT (FRESH BERRIES, MELONS, KIWI,
    PAPAYA, MANGO, ORANGES, ETC.)
1 CUP DICED POUND CAKE
4 SPRIGS FRESH MINT FOR GARNISH

1. Place the heavy cream in a mixing bowl and whisk to stiff peaks.

2. Fold in the vanilla yogurt and lemon curd. Keep refrigerated until serving.

3. Just before serving, gather four footed glass trifle cups (many glasses will do,
   e.g., martini glasses, large snifters) and divide half of the lemon mousse
   between the four glasses. Top the mousse with half of the granola, half of the
   fruit and half of the pound cake. Repeat this process with the remaining
   ingredients and garnish with a fresh mint sprig.

*Trifles are usually dessert fare, but the yogurt-based mousse creates a light and refreshing trifle more appropriate for breakfast. A good quality store-bought lemon curd can be used in place of my citrus curd to save time. For breakfast at the Inn, I have countless variations on this trifle. In place of the pound cake, try lemon-poppy seed bread or zucchini bread. Other alternatives include using a flavored yogurt in place of the mousse or layering in various fruit purees.* ■

## CRANBERRY AND APPLE CRUNCH FRENCH TOAST

SERVES 4

2 TABLESPOONS UNSALTED BUTTER
1 GRANNY SMITH APPLE
¼ CUP DRIED CRANBERRIES
2 TEASPOONS LIGHT BROWN SUGAR, FIRMLY PACKED
½ TEASPOON APPLE PIE SPICE MIX (RECIPE, PAGE 58)
1 LOAF FRENCH BREAD
3 EGGS
¼ CUP HEAVY CREAM
2 TEASPOONS APPLE PIE SPICE MIX
2 CUPS CORNFLAKES CEREAL
¼ CUP CHOPPED DRIED APPLES
2 TABLESPOONS UNSALTED BUTTER
POWDERED SUGAR IN SHAKER
WHIPPED CREAM

1. Melt the butter in a medium-sized sauté pan over medium heat. Peel and core the apple and cut into a ¼-inch dice. Sauté the apple cubes in the butter for 1 minute and add the dried cranberries, brown sugar and apple pie spice mix. Continue to cook for 1 minute, melting the sugar. Cover to keep warm and reserve.

2. Slice the French bread on an angle into twelve 1-inch-thick slices.

3. Combine the eggs, heavy cream and apple pie spice mix in a medium-sized mixing bowl and whisk to combine well.

4. In another medium-sized mixing bowl, combine the cornflakes and chopped

---

*One taste of this French toast and you'll never go back to the traditional soft and limp variety. The apple and cranberry mixture is great in the fall and really complements the crunch on the bread. Another combination that works well with the crunchy French toast is fresh (or frozen) peaches with a sweetened, whipped cream cheese. For a tropical twist, sauté banana slices in a little butter, add some brown sugar, crushed cashews and some shredded coconut, and serve over the crunchy French toast. ∎*

*A myriad of waffle irons are available on the market, each producing a waffle of a different shape or size. There are thin waffles, thick Belgian-style waffles, round waffles, square waffles, even heart-shaped waffles. They all work well so choose the type and shape you like. When serving waffles, dust the top with powdered sugar, add a dollop of sweetened, whipped cream and top with a garnish that will complement the flavoring of the waffles; try banana slices and halved walnuts on the banana-walnut waffles, for example. ▪*

dried apples. Crumble the cornflakes with your hands until they are broken down to the size of peas.

5. Dunk the bread, a few pieces at a time, into the egg mixture. Allow it to soak up some of the egg mixture for 10 seconds and transfer to the crumb mixture to coat each side.

6. Melt the butter in a large sauté pan set over medium heat. Toast the coated bread slices on each side until lightly golden brown.

7. To serve, arrange three slices of the French toast on each plate. Dust with powdered sugar and divide the cranberry and apple mixture between the plates, placing it on top of the toast. Top with a dollop of whipped cream and serve with pure Maine maple syrup and a side of your favorite breakfast meat.

# WAFFLES

SERVES 4

1 CUP ALL-PURPOSE FLOUR
1 TEASPOON BAKING POWDER
1 TABLESPOON POWDERED SUGAR
1/2 TABLESPOON CANOLA OIL
1 CUP MILK
1 EGG, SEPARATED
1 TEASPOON VANILLA EXTRACT
PINCH KOSHER SALT
VEGETABLE PAN COATING

1. Mix the flour, baking powder and powdered sugar together in a mixing bowl.

2. Add the oil, milk, egg yolk, vanilla and salt and mix until smooth.

3. Choose from the waffle flavors on the opposite page, and stir the ingredients into the batter, mixing well.

4. Whip the egg white to stiff peaks and fold into the batter.

5. Heat the waffle iron and coat with a layer of vegetable pan coating. Ladle in the waffle batter and cook until crisp, following the manufacturer's recommended techniques and settings.

BLUEBERRY-ALMOND: ¼ cup blueberries and 2 Tablespoons toasted sliced almonds

PUMPKIN SPICE: ½ cup pumpkin puree, ½ teaspoon cinnamon, ¼ teaspoon each: nutmeg, ginger and allspice

GINGERBREAD: 1 Tablespoon dark molasses, ½ teaspoon cinnamon, ¼ teaspoon allspice, ¼ teaspoon ground cloves

LEMON-POPPY SEED: 1 Tablespoon fresh lemon juice, 1 teaspoon lemon extract, 1 teaspoon grated lemon zest and 1 teaspoon poppy seeds

BANANA-WALNUT: 1 chopped ripe banana and 2 Tablespoons chopped walnuts

BIRDSEED: 2 teaspoons each: sunflower seeds, sesame seeds, poppy seeds and chopped up pumpkin seeds

## CREAM HORNS WITH CITRUS CURD

SERVES 6

1/2 SHEET PUFF PASTRY (HOMEMADE OR YOUR FAVORITE BRAND)
VEGETABLE PAN COATING
1 EGG, BEATEN
1/4 TEASPOON GROUND CINNAMON
1 TEASPOON GRANULATED SUGAR
1/2 BATCH OF CITRUS CURD (RECIPE FOLLOWS)
3 CUPS CHOPPED FRESH FRUIT (FRESH BERRIES, MELONS, KIWI, PAPAYA, MANGO, ORANGES, ETC.)

*Cream horn molds are not your standard kitchen tool but the presentation of this dish makes it worth the investment. Alternatively, you can cut the puff pastry into various shapes, round, rectangular, triangular, or, with a cookie cutter, into a shape of your choice, and then bake following the same directions in Step 4. Other fillings that work well in the cream horn are pastry cream, flavored whipped cream or fruit mousses.* ■

POWDERED SUGAR IN SHAKER
½ CUP CRÈME ANGLAISE (OPTIONAL, RECIPE, PAGE 40)

1. For this recipe you will need 6 cream horn molds, which are basically cone-shaped pieces of metal (sometimes Teflon coated) that you wrap the pastry around to achieve the cone-shaped "horns." Once the pastry has cooled, you remove the molds from the inside of the pastries.

2. Preheat the oven to 350 degrees.

3. Place the puff pastry on the work counter and cut into rectangular strips 1½ inches by 12 inches long. Spray the cream horn molds with a light layer of the vegetable pan coating and wrap the pastry strips around the cream horn molds. Start at the tip of the cone and make one turn, being sure to pinch the end of the strip to secure it. Continue rolling the pastry up the cone, slightly overlapping and sealing each wrap over the previous one.

4. Place the wrapped molds on a parchment- or Silpat-lined baking sheet and lightly brush the exposed tops with the beaten egg. Combine the cinnamon and sugar and mix well. Sprinkle over the cream horns and place the sheet in the preheated oven to bake for 20 minutes, or until golden brown. Cool.

5. To serve, remove the molds from the horns and fill with the citrus curd. Lay the cream horns on the plates and arrange the chopped fruit around the plate. Dust with powdered sugar and surround with a small pool of crème Anglaise, if desired. Serve immediately before the pastry gets soggy.

## CITRUS CURD

MAKES 3 CUPS OF CURD

1$^1$/$_2$ CUPS GRANULATED SUGAR
1 ORANGE
$^1$/$_2$ LEMON
$^1$/$_2$ LIME
$^1$/$_2$ POUND (8 TABLESPOONS) UNSALTED BUTTER, SOFT
5 EGGS
PINCH KOSHER SALT

1. Place the sugar in a medium-sized saucepan.

2. Finely zest the orange, half lemon and half lime and mix the zest in with the sugar. Cut each fruit in half and squeeze out all of the juice, and reserve.

3. Add the soft butter to the pan and mix it in well. Add the eggs, one at a time, and mix until combined. Mix in the reserved citrus juice and salt.

4. Place the saucepan over medium heat, stirring occasionally, until thickened (brought to 175 degrees). *Cool and keep refrigerated for up to 2 weeks.*

5. For a plain lemon curd, use 2 lemons and omit the orange and lime.

# APPLE TARTS

SERVES 6

1 SHEET PUFF PASTRY (HOMEMADE OR YOUR FAVORITE BRAND)
VEGETABLE PAN COATING
1 EGG, BEATEN
6 Tablespoons ALMOND PASTE
1½ GRANNY SMITH APPLES
2 Tablespoons GRANULATED SUGAR
1½ teaspoons APPLE PIE SPICE MIX (RECIPE FOLLOWS)
POWDERED SUGAR IN SHAKER
1 CUP CRÈME ANGLAISE (RECIPE, PAGE 40)
6 SCOOPS VANILLA ICE CREAM

1. Preheat the oven to 350 degrees.

2. Lay out the puff pastry dough and cut into six 3-inch circles (a scalloped 3-inch cutter works well).

3. Lightly coat a baking sheet with vegetable spray and lay the pastry circles on top. Brush the pastry with the beaten egg and place 1 Tablespoon of almond paste in the center of each pastry round.

4. Cut the whole apple in half and core all three halves with a melon baller. Slice each apple half from top to bottom into very thin slices, keeping them together.

5. Separate each sliced apple half into two equal halves and spread out one equal half per pastry circle, leaving a border around the outside. If you start by laying down the cut side of the apple half first and fanning the rest on top, the apple will conform to the round shape of the pastry. One apple will make four tarts.

*This simple tart recipe is great with many fresh fruits. In place of the apple slices, try strawberry halves, pear slices, nectarine or skinless peach halves or mango slices. To skin a peach, cut a shallow "x" in the bottom of a peach and immerse the peach into boiling water for 30 seconds. Remove immediately to a bath of ice water to cool and peel the skin from the peach with a paring knife, starting at the points created by the cuts in the bottom. ■*

6. Mix together 2 Tablespoons sugar with ½ teaspoon apple pie spice mix and sprinkle an even coating on top of each tart.

7. Bake in the preheated oven for about 35 minutes, or until golden brown.

8. Make a spiced crème Anglaise by combining the sauce with 1 teaspoon of the apple pie spice mix.

9. Serve on a plate dusted with powdered sugar, surrounded by a pool of spiced crème Anglaise and a scoop of vanilla ice cream.

## APPLE PIE SPICE MIX

3 TABLESPOONS GROUND CINNAMON
1½ TABLESPOONS GROUND GINGER
2 TEASPOONS GROUND NUTMEG
2 TEASPOONS GROUND ALLSPICE
1 TEASPOON GROUND CARDAMOM

I. Mix all of the spices together and keep in a tightly covered jar in a dark place.

# MICHAEL'S ITALIAN BREAKFAST SAUSAGE

### YIELDS ABOUT 8 PATTIES

1 POUND GROUND PORK
2 TABLESPOONS FENNEL SPICE MIX (RECIPE FOLLOWS)
1½ TABLESPOONS DRY WHITE WINE
8 THICK SLICES OF SPECIALTY SMOKED BACON (OPTIONAL)
CANOLA OIL

1. Mix the ingredients together until well combined.

2. Form into small patties. (Optional: Wrap the patties with a slice of bacon.)

3. Heat a sauté pan over medium heat. Add some canola oil and cook for 3 minutes on each side or until browned and cooked through. Bacon-wrapped patties take more time to cook and should be finished in a preheated 350-degree oven for 10 minutes.

## FENNEL SPICE MIX

2 TABLESPOONS WHOLE FENNEL SEEDS, TOASTED AND GROUND
1 TABLESPOON GROUND BLACK PEPPER
1 TABLESPOON GRANULATED GARLIC
2 1/2 TABLESPOONS KOSHER SALT

1. Place the whole fennel seeds in a small sauté pan and toss over medium-high heat until fragrant and lightly toasted. Finely grind in a spice grinder.

2. Mix all of the ingredients together until well combined. Store in a jar with a tightly sealed lid.

## SMOKED TURKEY BREAKFAST WRAP WITH HOLLANDAISE

SERVES 4

8 EGGS
1/4 CUP MILK
1/4 TEASPOON KOSHER SALT
PINCH OF WHITE PEPPER
2 TABLESPOONS UNSALTED BUTTER
2 TEASPOONS OLIVE OIL

*Breakfast wraps are a great way to add variety to the breakfast table. Tortillas are available in so many terrific flavors these days that the hardest part of this recipe is choosing between the garlic-herb tortillas and the sun-dried tomato and basil tortillas. Ham, prosciutto and bacon can all be used in place of the smoked turkey and, of course, any type of cheese may be used. I like to add grilled vegetables to the inside of the wraps as well. If you don't want to make hollandaise, try it with my secret sauce from the first cookbook.* ▪

4 FLAVORED FLOUR TORTILLAS (GARLIC-HERB, SPINACH,
    TOMATO-BASIL, ETC.)
4 TABLESPOONS SOUR CREAM
1/2 CUP SHREDDED SWISS CHEESE
8 SLICES SMOKED TURKEY BREAST
1 BATCH HOLLANDAISE SAUCE (RECIPE, PAGE 156)

1. Preheat the oven to 350 degrees.

2. Crack the eggs into a medium-sized bowl and whisk until well blended. Add the milk and whisk to combine. Season with the salt and white pepper.

3. Heat a medium-sized nonstick pan over medium-high heat. Add the butter and melt. Add the eggs and scramble until just cooked through. Remove from the pan.

4. Heat a large sauté pan over medium-high heat and add ½ teaspoon of the olive oil. Warm a tortilla on each side in the oil, toasting it lightly, and remove to a foil-lined baking sheet. Continue with the other tortillas and oil.

5. Spread a Tablespoon of sour cream over ⅔ of each tortilla, leaving the furthest side from you and the edges on each side without sour cream. Sprinkle the Swiss cheese on the sour cream and top with two slices of smoked turkey breast.

6. Divide the cooked scrambled eggs between the tortillas, placing the eggs on the front center portion of the turkey breast. Roll the tortilla over the scrambled eggs and continue to roll halfway. Fold the two sides in on the middle of the tortilla to close the sides, and continue the roll to complete the wrap.

7. Place the wraps back on the foil-lined baking sheet and bake in the preheated oven for 15 minutes to warm through. Slice the wrap in half on the diagonal and serve with the hollandaise sauce.

# Camden Windjammer Weekend

DURING THE EARLY 1800S, Camden was known for its shipbuilding, so it is only fitting that most of Maine's stately windjammer fleet, with sails billowing and decks polished, gathers in Camden Harbor for the annual Camden Windjammer Weekend. Held every Labor Day weekend, this lively tall ships festival honors the days when hundreds of coastal schooners lined Maine's harbors.

Early Friday afternoon, join the crowd and watch as the *Surprise*, the *Mary Day, Lewis R French, Nathaniel Bowditch, Isaac H. Evans*, and so many more, maneuver picturesque Camden Harbor with ease and grace. Take the opportunity to see the majestic *Victory Chimes*, the only original three-masted schooner in the famed Maine windjammer fleet. It was built in 1900, and is 127.5 feet long, with masts over 80 feet in height. Beautiful *Grace Bailey*, built in 1882 and 123 feet long, is also listed as a National Landmark. *Stephen Taber*, 115 feet long, was built in 1871 and, along with many others, is a tribute to American schooner craftsmanship. Some of these vessels are powered by wind and canvas alone. Their broad wooden decks remind you that these are authentic 19th- and 20th-century sailing ships.

Friday night, enjoy a fun-filled Schooner Bum Talent Show put on by their crew and passengers, and afterward, a rousing display of fireworks. Over the weekend, there's also a flag raising ceremony, blessing of the fleet, a stunning parade of sail and cruises. There's much more to see and do. You can take onboard tours of participating

windjammers that, depending on their size, accommodate anywhere between six and forty passengers, participate in the build-a-boat competition and race, a Chowder Challenge where your vote counts, sea music workshops and a sing-along, the popular Harbor Hounds Dog Show, and more. "Captain's Courageous" plays for free at the Bay View Street Cinema and schooner crew cooks display their talents in the Schooner Pie Baking Contest. Sunday night, kick back at the Harbor Park Concert and then watch the windjammers depart to a lighted boat and brass trio send-off.

Quite simply, the Camden Windjammer Weekend is a delightful way to bid farewell to the late summer breezes of Penobscot Bay, where sailing has and continues to be an exceptional and dramatic experience. ■

Afternoon Tea
& Cookies

# Flourless Nut and Chocolate Chunk Cookies

*Jody Schmoll, a friend and former Camden innkeeper, gave me a recipe for her flourless peanut butter cookies. I took her base recipe and embellished it with lots of nuts and some chocolate chunks and came up with these cookies. The first time I tasted them, I unanimously proclaimed these as my new favorite cookies. This cookie dough is quite coarse and when you make the balls, they may need a little extra effort to get them to hold together, but they are well worth it.* ∎

### MAKES 40 COOKIES

2 CUPS CHUNKY PEANUT BUTTER
2 CUPS GRANULATED SUGAR
2 TEASPOONS BAKING POWDER
2 EGGS
1/2 CUP SLICED ALMONDS
1/2 CUP WALNUT PIECES
1/2 CUP SALTED PEANUTS, LIGHTLY CRUSHED
1/2 CUP CHOCOLATE CHUNKS (DARK OR WHITE CHOCOLATE)

1. Preheat the oven to 350 degrees.

2. Cream together the peanut butter, sugar and baking powder. Stir in the eggs and mix well.

3. Fold in the nuts and chocolate chunks and mix to combine; the mixture will be quite coarse.

4. Make balls with a #40 ice cream scoop and place about 2 inches apart on a baking sheet lined with a nonstick baking mat or on a lightly greased baking sheet. Press down a little and sprinkle the top with coarse baking sugar.

5. Bake for 15 minutes. Transfer the cookies to cooling racks to cool completely.

# ℒEMON-POPPY SEED COOKIES

### MAKES 25 COOKIES

1 CUP (16 TABLESPOONS) UNSALTED BUTTER, SOFT
1 CUP GRANULATED SUGAR
2 1/4 CUPS ALL-PURPOSE FLOUR
1 TEASPOON BAKING POWDER
1/2 TEASPOON KOSHER SALT
1 TABLESPOON POPPY SEEDS
1 EGG
2 TEASPOONS VANILLA EXTRACT
1 LEMON, JUICE AND ZEST
GRANULATED SUGAR FOR COATING

*These tart, thin cookies are perfect with tea service. I have tried them with other citrus fruit as well and tangerine-poppy seed are also a favorite.* ■

1. Preheat the oven to 350 degrees.

2. Cream together the butter and sugar until fluffy.

3. In another bowl, mix together the flour, baking powder, salt and poppy seeds.

4. Add the egg to the creamed butter and mix in well. Add the vanilla, lemon juice and lemon zest and mix until combined.

5. Slowly add the flour mixture to the wet mixture and mix just until the dough forms.

6. Make balls with a #40 ice cream scoop and place about 2 inches apart on a baking sheet lined with a nonstick baking mat or on a lightly greased baking sheet. Sprinkle the cookie balls with granulated sugar and press them down with the flat bottom of a glass until 1/4 inch thick.

7. Bake for 13 minutes. Transfer the cookies to cooling racks to cool completely.

# ALMOND MACAROONS

MAKES 15 COOKIES

1 POUND ALMOND PASTE (ABOUT 1 CUP)
2 CUPS GRANULATED SUGAR
4 LARGE EGGS, WHITES ONLY
GRANULATED SUGAR FOR SPRINKLING

1. Preheat the oven to 375 degrees.

2. Place the almond paste in a food processor with the sugar. Process until well blended. While the food processor is on, add the egg whites gradually and blend until well combined.

3. Line a cookie sheet with a Silpat mat or parchment paper. Make balls with a #40 ice cream scoop and place about 2 inches apart on the lined baking sheet.

4. Sprinkle the cookies lightly with the granulated sugar and bake in the preheated oven for 18 to 20 minutes or until lightly browned. Remove from the oven and cool on the sheet. Use a spatula to remove the cookies from the sheet.

*I love macaroons, whether they are made from coconut or almonds. These cookies are crisp on the outside and soft in the middle and are very easy to make. Almond paste is available in most grocery stores and is made of equal parts of ground almonds and powdered sugar. Don't confuse almond paste with marzipan, which has a much higher sugar content and less true almond flavor.* ■

# Macadamia and Caramel Cookies

MAKES 40 COOKIES

1 CUP UNSALTED BUTTER, SOFT
1 CUP GRANULATED SUGAR
1/2 CUP LIGHT BROWN SUGAR, FIRMLY PACKED
2 LARGE EGGS
1 TEASPOON VANILLA EXTRACT
3 CUPS ALL-PURPOSE FLOUR
2 TEASPOONS BAKING POWDER
1 TEASPOON KOSHER SALT
1 CUP COARSELY GROUND TOASTED MACADAMIA NUTS
3/4 CUP CHOPPED SOFT CARAMEL CANDIES
3/4 CUP WHITE CHOCOLATE CHIPS

1. Preheat the oven to 350 degrees.

2. Cream together the butter and sugars in a mixer. Add the eggs and vanilla extract and mix well.

3. In a separate bowl, combine the flour, baking powder and salt and mix well.

4. Slowly add the flour mixture to the butter and sugar mixture and combine well.

5. Gently stir in the macadamia nuts, chopped caramels and white chocolate chips.

6. Make balls with a #40 ice cream scoop and place about 2 inches apart on a baking sheet lined with a nonstick baking mat or on a lightly greased baking sheet.

7. Bake for 18 minutes. Remove from the oven and after 5 minutes, transfer them to a cooling rack until they cool completely.

*Macadamia nuts and caramel is one of my favorite combinations. The macadamia tree is native to eastern Australia but Hawaii is the largest commercial producer of the nut. The outside shell of the nut is very hard and thin and requires about 300 psi to crack it. Another note of interest to pet owners is the fact that macadamia nuts are toxic to dogs, so keep them away from Fido.* ■

# COFFEE SNAPS

MAKES 36 COOKIES

1 CUP (16 TABLESPOONS) UNSALTED BUTTER
2 CUPS LIGHT BROWN SUGAR, FIRMLY PACKED
3 TABLESPOONS INSTANT COFFEE
2 TEASPOONS VANILLA EXTRACT
2 EGGS
3 CUPS ALL-PURPOSE FLOUR
2 TEASPOONS BAKING POWDER
3 TABLESPOONS WHOLE COFFEE BEANS

1. Preheat the oven to 350 degrees.

2. Cream together the butter, sugar, instant coffee and vanilla extract.

3. Stir in the eggs and mix well.

4. Mix the flour and baking powder together and slowly add them to the butter mixture. Stir until well combined.

5. Make balls with a #40 ice cream scoop and place about 2 inches apart on a baking sheet lined with a nonstick baking mat or on a lightly greased baking sheet. Press a whole coffee bean into the top of each cookie.

6. Bake for 14 minutes. Transfer the cookies to cooling racks to cool completely.

*Cookies are often served with coffee, so why not combine the two together. Of course you can still have coffee on the side. These cookies pack a real strong coffee flavor and the crunch from the whole coffee bean on top is a special and unexpected treat.* ■

# Double Chocolate-Cranberry Biscotti

MAKES 40 COOKIES

2 3/4 CUPS ALL-PURPOSE FLOUR
1 1/2 CUPS GRANULATED SUGAR
2 1/2 TEASPOONS BAKING POWDER
1/2 CUP COCOA POWDER
1 TEASPOON KOSHER SALT
1/2 CUP (8 TABLESPOONS) UNSALTED BUTTER, CHILLED AND CUT
    INTO SMALL PIECES
2 LARGE EGGS
1/4 CUP CRÈME DE CACAO (LIQUEUR)
2 TEASPOONS ALMOND EXTRACT
6 OUNCES DARK CHOCOLATE, MEDIUM-COARSE CHOP
1 1/2 CUPS WHOLE PISTACHIOS, TOASTED AND COARSELY CHOPPED
6 OUNCES DRIED CRANBERRIES

1. Line a baking sheet with a nonstick baking mat or a piece of foil that has been buttered and floured.

2. Combine the flour, sugar, baking powder, cocoa powder and salt in the bowl of a food processor. Pulse a few times to combine the ingredients. Add the butter and process until a fine meal forms.

3. In a large bowl, beat the eggs, crème de cacao and almond extract. Add the flour mixture and stir to combine. Add the dark chocolate, pistachios and dried cranberries and stir until a moist dough forms.

*Chocolate cookies are always a big hit at the Inn and these twice-baked Italian favorites are no exception. Packed with cocoa powder, crème de cacao and chocolate chunks, this recipe is a variation on the almond and apricot biscotti from my first cookbook. Some of my other favorite flavors and combinations for biscotti include orange-raisin, anisette, vanilla-hazelnut and peanut butter-chocolate chunk.* ■

4. Divide the dough in thirds and form into three logs on the prepared sheet, spacing them evenly. Moisten fingertips and shape each log into a 3 inches wide by 10 inches long rectangular strip. Cover with plastic wrap and refrigerate for 30 minutes, or until the dough is firm.

5. Position the rack in the center of the oven and preheat the oven to 350 degrees.

6. Bake until the logs are golden brown, about 30 minutes. Transfer sheet to a rack and cool completely. Reduce oven temperature to 300 degrees.

7. Remove the logs from the sheet and transfer to a cutting board. Using a serrated knife, carefully cut each log crosswise into ¾-inch-wide slices. Arrange the cookies, cut side down, on two baking sheets with parchment paper. Bake for 10 minutes. Gently turn the cookies over and bake 10 minutes longer. Transfer cookies to cooling racks and cool completely. *Biscotti keep well for 2 to 3 weeks if stored in an airtight container at room temperature. They also freeze well.*

# Coconut-Chocolate Macaroons

MAKES 15 COOKIES

4 LARGE EGGS, WHITES ONLY
1/4 CUP GRANULATED SUGAR
1 TEASPOON VANILLA EXTRACT
1/2 TEASPOON ALMOND EXTRACT
1/8 TEASPOON KOSHER SALT
3 CUPS SWEETENED FLAKED COCONUT
4 OUNCES DARK CHOCOLATE

1. Preheat the oven to 325 degrees.

2. In a medium-sized mixing bowl, combine the egg whites, sugar, both extracts and the salt. Stir to combine. Stir in the coconut.

3. Make balls with a #40 ice cream scoop and place about 2 inches apart on a Silpat-lined baking sheet or on a lightly greased baking sheet.

4. Bake for 18–20 minutes or until the macaroons start to turn lightly golden. Allow the cookies to cool for 5 minutes and transfer them to cooling racks to cool completely.

5. Coarsely chop the chocolate and put it in a small glass (microwave proof) bowl. Melt the chocolate in the microwave for 30 seconds at a time, stirring after each interval, until the chocolate is completely melted. Drizzle the chocolate over the cooled cookies and allow the chocolate to set up before moving them.

6. Keep in an airtight container.

*Coconut lovers beware. I drizzle these cookies with chocolate at the Inn, but true chocoholics may want to go one step further. Melt one pound of chocolate as instructed in Step 5 and dip the cookies completely in the chocolate. Use a fork to retrieve the cookie and drain off excess chocolate. Set the coated macaroons on a parchment-lined baking sheet and allow the chocolate to harden in a cool place.* ■

# Christmas
### by the
## Sea

COME TO MAINE and experience your own winter wonderland during "Christmas by the Sea." This annual three-day celebration is held the first weekend in December in Camden, Rockport and Lincolnville, and offers something for everyone. With much holiday spirit, many local businesses and organizations sponsor a myriad of festivities that embrace what it means to enjoy an old-fashioned Christmas the Maine way.

The "Christmas by the Sea" parade signals the beginning of the weekend festivities and culminates with the Community Tree Lighting in Harbor Park, where all gather to enjoy the sparkling lights, sing carols and warm up with hot cocoa. Santa heads the parade but makes his grand appearance Saturday morning when he arrives by Lobster Boat in Rockport Harbor first and then Camden Harbor. It's a full day for Santa. He reads a special Christmas story to young and old in the Camden Public Library in the early afternoon, has free photos taken with children and eventually finds his way, quite easily for him — after all, he is Santa Claus — to Lincolnville Beach for evening festivities, including a gala bonfire.

In addition, "Christmas by the Sea" offers a live Nativity scene one can stroll through or carriage rides one can bundle up in or Aldemere Farm, where one can make beltie

calf (the "Oreo" cookie cow) ornaments. The downtown shops in Camden run a 10 to 20 percent off sale and remain open well into the night. Strolling carolers can be heard up and down the downtown streets. "It's a Wonderful Life" plays for free at the Bay View Street Cinema, Christmas concerts abound, and yes, there's a live production of *The Nutcracker*. There's actually more to do than anyone can pack in. Half the fun is picking and choosing what appeals to you most.

Most of all, though, "Christmas by the Sea" is all about the Christmas spirit, and sharing it with family and friends the old-fashioned way right here in midcoast Maine. ∎

# Our Favorite Cocktails & Drinks

MARY JO AND I LOVE to try new cocktails during our travels. Once we are back at home, the chef in me wants to figure out the recipe and perfect it. Mary Jo is quite a critic when it comes to this process and she doesn't let me rest until I get it right.

Specialty cocktails are a terrific way to start a dinner party, whether it is a small gathering for hors d'oeuvres or a more elaborate dinner event. Typically, we will choose one cocktail for the evening and have it mixed up and ready to go as the guests arrive. I have chosen some of our favorite cocktails to include in this book because they are such an important component in the execution of the perfect dining experience.

Aperitifs (before dinner drinks) — Bellinis are a very simple way to transform sparkling wine into something even more special. There is a canned bellini mix available on the market that is very good and simplifies the process. Cosmopolitans are quite refreshing and at their best when made with fresh lime juice. I refuse to order them at a bar that uses bottled juice. Mojitos are fun and a great way to use some of the fresh mint that thrives in my garden. Other fresh berries can also be used if blackberries are not available or try it the traditional way without any berries at all. For those who are feeling tropical, try the frozen mango margarita, and of course, any fresh fruit can be used in place of the mango.

Cordials (after dinner drinks) — Limoncello is an Italian cordial that is very sweet and concentrated in flavor. The process of making limoncello is a bit lengthy, but good things are worth waiting for. I suggest that you go out and buy a bottle of Italian limoncello while yours is developing and conduct a taste test once your homemade limoncello is complete. For a stronger drink, grain alcohol can be used in place of the vodka. Café Diablo (devil's coffee) is a strong coffee drink consumed at the end of a meal. In Aruba, I used to prepare this coffee tableside (dim the lights) in an elaborate ceremony where the flames would climb their way up a long spiraled orange rind and the cinnamon dust would light up in sparks.

# OSMOPOLITAN

1½ LIMES
¼ CUP CRANBERRY JUICE (OR POMEGRANATE JUICE)
¼ CUP TRIPLE SEC
½ CUP VODKA
1 CUP CRUSHED ICE
STRIPS OF LIME PEEL FOR GARNISH

1. Juice the limes and mix the lime juice, cranberry juice, triple sec and vodka together in a cocktail shaker.

2. Add the crushed ice, secure the top of the shaker and shake vigorously for 20 seconds.

3. Strain the drink into 2 chilled martini glasses and garnish with a strip of lime peel.

*I am always so disappointed when I order this drink at a bar and they make it with bottled lime juice. It is so much better with fresh lime juice. There are many variations on this drink; try flavored vodkas with different juice combinations, like Razmapolitan with raspberry vodka and a splash of raspberry puree, Peachmapolitan with peach vodka and peach juice or puree.* ■

*The mojito is a traditional Cuban drink that is sweet and refreshing, with a rum kick. All summer long my herb garden is taken over with a huge patch of spearmint and I couldn't be happier about it. As one of our most popular drink specials, the mojito is delicious on its own or with the addition of berries or other fruits. The blackberries make for a dramatic presentation.* ■

# BLACKBERRY MOJITO

1/2 CUP FRESH MINT LEAVES
4 TEASPOONS GRANULATED SUGAR (OR 2 PACKETS OF SPLENDA)
2 LIMES
1/4 CUP FRESH BLACKBERRIES
3/4 CUP LIGHT RUM
1 CUP CLUB SODA
2 SPRIGS FRESH MINT FOR GARNISH

1. Place the mint and sugar in a mortar and "muddle" it with a pestle. Squeeze in the lime juice and add half of the blackberries. Lightly crush the berries.

2. Pour the mixture into a cocktail shaker and add the light rum and club soda. Shake to mix.

3. Place 4 large cubes of ice in two rocks glasses and divide the drink equally between them.

4. Garnish each glass with the remaining blackberries and a sprig of fresh mint.

# Key Lime Martini

GRAHAM CRACKER CRUMBS
1¹/₂ LIMES
³/₄ CUP KeKe BEACH LIQUEUR
³/₈ CUP VANILLA VODKA
1 CUP CRUSHED ICE

1. Make a thin layer of graham cracker crumbs on a small plate. Juice the limes and reserve the juice for Step 2 below. Take one of the lime halves and coat the rim of two martini glasses with lime juice. Invert the glass and dip the rim in the graham cracker crumbs to coat the rim. Place the glasses in the freezer to frost them.

2. Mix the lime juice, KeKe Beach liqueur and vanilla vodka together in a cocktail shaker.

3. Add the crushed ice, secure the top of the shaker and shake vigorously for 20 seconds.

4. Strain the drink into 2 chilled martini glasses and serve immediately.

*The key to this drink is the use of KeKe Beach liqueur. If you can't find this unique liqueur, I have another recipe compliments of my friend Bert Witham: 3 parts vanilla vodka, 2 parts midori, 1 part lime juice and a splash of cream. In Maine, we don't see true key limes very often, but when we do, I will most certainly use them in these cocktails as they are more flavorful and sour. ■*

*Mary Jo and I spent three lovely years living on the island of Aruba. With a fresh fruit and vegetable market on the side of the road on our way home from work, we would often stop and get tropical fruit for cold blended drinks. This was one of our favorite drinks on those hot tropical nights. Papayas, strawberries and peaches also work well as margarita flavors. ▪*

# Frozen Mango Margarita

1 RIPE MANGO, PEELED, DESEEDED AND ROUGHLY CHOPPED
   (RESERVE 2 SLICES FOR GARNISH)
2 LIMES, CUT IN HALF (RESERVE 2 THIN SLICES FOR GARNISH)
1/2 CUP TEQUILA
1/4 CUP TRIPLE SEC
3 CUPS CRUSHED ICE

1. Combine the mango, squeezed lime juice, tequila and triple sec in a blender and blend until smooth.

2. Add the crushed ice and blend until smooth.

3. Divide the drink between two hurricane glasses (or other large cocktail glasses) and garnish with the lime and mango slices.

# ℒIMONCELLO

15 LEMONS
2 BOTTLES VODKA (100 PROOF), 750 ML EACH
4 CUPS GRANULATED SUGAR
1¹/₂ QUARTS WATER

1. Wash the lemons with hot water. Using a vegetable peeler, remove the skin from the lemons. Reserve the lemon juice for other recipes. Remove the white pith from the lemon peels with a kitchen knife, leaving only strips of the bright yellow skin.

2. Place the lemon peels in a large (at least 1 gallon) glass jar and cover with the contents from one bottle of vodka. Seal the jar tightly and store in a cool dark place for one month.

3. After the month has passed, make a simple syrup by combining the sugar and water in a saucepan and bringing it to a boil. Simmer for about 10 minutes, stirring in all of the sugar crystals from the side of the pan, and dissolving all of the sugar. Cool completely. Add the simple syrup to the jar with the lemon vodka along with the remaining bottle of vodka, stir and seal tightly. Return the jar to the cool dark place for another month.

4. After the final month has passed, strain the liquid from the lemon peels and store in bottles in the freezer. Serve the limoncello very cold in small chilled glasses.

*Limoncello is a lemon liqueur produced in the south of Italy. Various regions in Italy use different types of lemons to create liqueurs with subtle differences. Making limoncello at home is a lengthy process, but it is well worth the effort. It takes two months from beginning to end, but the process is quite simple. A few variations worth noting are the use of lime, mandarin or tangerine skin in place of the lemon. If you can get pure grain alcohol, it can also be used in place of the vodka for a more pure lemon flavor.* ■

ELLINI

¹/4 CUP WHITE PEACH PUREE (FRESH OR CANNED)
PROSECO (ITALIAN SPARKLING WINE) OR CHAMPAGNE
FRESH PEACH SLICES FOR GARNISH

1. Divide the peach puree between two Champagne flutes. Top off with sparkling wine or Champagne.

2. Garnish with a fresh peach slice.

## AFÉ DIABLO

¹/4 CUP GRANULATED SUGAR
2 TABLESPOONS WATER
1 TEASPOON FINELY GRATED ORANGE ZEST
2 TEASPOONS BRANDY
1 TABLESPOON GRAND MARNIER
2 TABLESPOONS KAHLUA
2 TABLESPOONS AMARETTO
2 TABLESPOONS FRANGELICO
2 TABLESPOONS BAILEYS IRISH CREAM
2 CUPS HOT STRONG COFFEE
DASH OF CINNAMON

1. Combine the sugar, water and orange zest in a medium-sized saucepan over high heat. Bring to a boil and simmer for 1 minute. Add the brandy and Grand Marnier to the pan and heat. Flame the brandy by lighting a long bamboo skewer and extending it carefully into the pan, being very careful not to burn yourself.

2. When the flame ceases, add the remaining liqueurs to the pan and heat to a simmer. Add the coffee and cinnamon, mix well and strain into serving glasses. Serve immediately.

*In some of the fancy restaurants I have worked in over the years, we used to prepare this drink tableside with lots of theatrics. We would flame the alcohol with lights dimmed, and ladle the flames high into the air. Endless spirals of orange rind would cascade with rings of fire, and simultaneously, we'd release clouds of cinnamon that would sparkle as they crossed paths with the flames. What a show! If you're going to try this at home, make sure to have a fire extinguisher nearby. ∎*

# Wine & Food

### by
### Joe Nardone

MANY PEOPLE have tried to capture the essence of wine in words, to describe what it is, how it tastes and its significance in the culinary world. Wine has been referred to a thousand different ways; it has been called bottled emotion and the embodiment of a place and time. Books have been written, panels convened, scores handed out and even movies produced, all to give homage to a beverage. An entire industry has been built on the simple question, "What should I drink with dinner tonight?" The answer to that question is whatever you like.

A friend of mine puts Tabasco sauce on everything — eggs, sandwiches, steaks, lobster. I believe she may even add it to several desserts. It is her condiment of choice. While it may not be the "appropriate" choice, she is willing to brave the stigma of culinary incorrectness because it is what she enjoys. This simple sentiment is what we tend to forget when we pontificate about food and wine. They are all about enjoyment. Food and wine are about flavors and friends, about camaraderie and colors, about memories and texture. It is okay to have a merlot with Chilean sea bass, and there is no law against enjoying a big, oaky chardonnay with filet mignon and feel free to drink Champagne with salted nuts and nachos. So why all the discussion about which wine with which food? Well, when Tabasco sauce is used with the appropriate dish it does add something to the flavor, it does make it better than what it was before. In the same way, wine is the ultimate condiment. It not only enhances the flavors of the food, but also the atmosphere, the company and the moment. The flavors it offers are endless and because of that it can add something to almost any dish. The trick, and the reason for all the discussion, is finding which flavors in both the food and the wine work best together. While there is no easy answer to this, there are some basic guidelines that can be followed.

First, decide whether the focus is on the food or the wine. While most dinner parties are about the food, there are some occasions when the wines are the focal point. If the occasion is about the wine, then choose a theme or concentrate on one varietal or region. If you would like to make the party a little more interesting, taste the wines while blindfolded. Choose one varietal, my favorite is chardonnay or sparkling wine, since

most people have already formed opinions on each of these. Select two or three very popular or highly regarded brands and then pick a few wines you have never heard of or may not think to try (white Burgundy for the chardonnay or Spanish sparkling wines are always fun). Wrap the bottles in bags or brightly colored tissue paper for a more festive look, and then number the bottles. Have your guests rate the wines from one to whatever number of wines you choose and at the end of the night reveal your top wines. The results may be surprising. At an event like this, the food should be simple — unseeded crackers and bread with a variety of cheeses, uncomplicated hors d'ouerves, antipasto or a mix of smoked meats and fish.

If your dinner party is about the food, and for me it usually is, then the wine choice requires a bit more thought. The old statement "white wine with fish, red wine with meat" is a good starting point. It should, however, be viewed more as a guideline than a rule. There are few times when all you are having is a simple piece of white fish or a nice steak on the grill without any sauce or sides. Menus are much more complicated and, therefore, our wine options need to expand. Several years ago a tasting was conducted in London. They invited more than 100 of Europe's top sommeliers to taste through a series of 12 wines. The stemware used in this tasting was made of black, opaque glass. Each participant was asked to taste through the wines, write down their impressions and then note what color they thought the wine was. While the tasting notes

from each of these wine experts were impeccable, only 50 percent of them were able to correctly identify which wines were red and which wines were white. The point being that the qualities of a particular wine are much more important than the actual color.

There are three basic characteristics of wine to look for when pairing it with food: relative dryness; acidity; and weight or richness.

Dry versus sweet. One of the most common statements you will hear is "I like a nice dry wine." Ninety percent of all the wine sold in the United States falls into the dry category (including riesling). Sweet wines are predominantly served with or for dessert or with a few select dishes; sauternes with foie gras comes to mind. The level of dryness can determine what to serve with a particular dish. A wine that is a little less dry, and thus a little lower in alcohol, is an excellent match for spicier foods. A drier wine, which in turn, will be a little heavier bodied can stand up to much heartier cuisine.

Acidity is that part of the wine that makes you pucker a little after a sip. But it is also the element of wine that makes it such a versatile condiment. A less acidic wine, which will taste rounder and richer, will soften more intense herbal or vegetal flavors in food. Higher acid wines will cut through the creaminess of a sauce or the fattier quality of meats.

Select lighter bodied wines to go with lighter fare and fuller bodied wines to pair with richer foods. Pinot grigio may be your wine of choice, but served with a hearty roast it will taste just like water.

Try to pick out the dominant flavors of any dish you may be having. Remember, flavor can come from the sauce or the herbs or from the preparation itself. Chicken is the perfect example. It can be cooked hundreds of ways, and depending on that preparation, it can demand any number of wine pairings.

Think about the origin of the dish. If you are having a classic northern Italian dish, then have a northern Italian wine. In most parts of the world, the wine culture grew around the culinary traditions of the region. They have spent hundreds of years doing the work for you and now produce only the wines that go with the food of that appellation.

Consider the setting. If you are dining at home with friends and everyone is having the same dish, then the pairing is much simpler. If you have several people ordering from a menu or are serving a variety of foods, then the wine choice needs to be much more versatile and a little less focused on any one flavor.

Don't be afraid. There are no right or wrong choices, you will not be ridiculed by your friends or blackballed from your favorite restaurant for choosing a wine that was not the perfect match. I assume that the reason you bought this cookbook is because you wanted to try something new, to expand your culinary awareness. So the next time you visit the Hartstone Inn, ask for a glass of that southern French red that you can't pronounce or grab a bottle of South African rosé from your favorite wine merchant. Taste what you don't know, and when that bit of doubt creeps in and you start to think, What if I don't like it, remember my friend, who is probably adding a dash of Tabasco to her apple cobbler and think as she does: This could be really great. ▪

*Appetizers*

# Antipasto

The Italian antipasto is typically a single component of lighter fare consumed at the beginning of a meal. The antipasto plate I prepare as an appetizer at the Inn is ever changing. I present between 5 to 7 very small portions of various antipasto-style dishes, some traditional and others a little more innovative. Arrange the various antipasto items on a single plate for a sit-down dinner or serve them on platters for a party or more informal type of gathering.

PROSCIUTTO-WRAPPED FRUIT: Sweet-ripe melons present a wonderful contrast to salty prosciutto. Simply wrap a thin slice of prosciutto around a thin wedge of melon that has been peeled. Cantaloupe, honeydew, Crenshaw or any ripe melon will do. Also try using other fruits like strawberries, kiwis and peaches.

GENOA SALAMI AND PROVOLONE ROLLS: Have the Genoa and provolone sliced very thin at the deli counter for the best results. Lay a slice of Genoa salami on the work surface in front of you and place a second slice on top, overlapping two-thirds of the first slice furthest from you. Lay a slice of provolone cheese on top of the salami and repeat the process again to make four layers in total. Starting nearest you, lift up and begin to roll the cheese and salami together into a tight roll. Gently press the roll with your hands to make the layers adhere and slice it in half on the bias to expose the spiral pattern.

GRILLED MARINATED MUSHROOMS: Any type of mushroom will work for this dish. The Italians, of course, use fresh porcini mushrooms, but they are hard to come by in the states. I use portobellas quite often but the standard button mushrooms also work well in this dish. Simply coat the cleaned mushrooms with olive oil and a sprinkle of kosher salt and freshly ground black pepper and grill in a hot grill pan for a few minutes. Large mushrooms should be cut into manageable bite-sized pieces. Place the mushrooms in a bowl and toss with a balsamic dressing made from 1 part balsamic vinegar, 3 parts extra virgin olive oil and add some fresh thyme, salt and pepper. Allow the mushrooms to marinate for at least 15 minutes.

GRILLED ZUCCHINI AND SHRIMP: Remove the ends of a cleaned zucchini and slice it on the bias into ½-inch-thick oval slices. Coat the slices with a drizzle of extra virgin olive oil and a sprinkling of kosher salt and freshly ground black pepper. For the shrimp I generally use a 16–20 count of tiger shrimp that has been peeled and deveined, leaving the fin tail on for presentation. Coat the shrimp with olive oil, salt and pepper and a little freshly minced garlic. Grill the zucchini and shrimp, marking them on both sides, and cooking the shrimp through. Serve the shrimp on top of the zucchini slices and drizzle with extra virgin olive oil.

PARMESAN CRISPS: Line a small baking sheet with a Silpat mat or parchment paper. Preheat the oven to 350 degrees. Make small thin piles (the size of a quarter) of freshly grated Parmesan cheese on the Silpat, spacing them 2 inches apart. Bake the crisps for about 18 minutes or until uniformly golden in color. Remove and immediately balance the crisps on a rolling pin or wine bottle while they are still hot to give them a slight curve for presentation.

BRUSCHETTA: Bruschetta is simply a grilled piece of crusty country-style bread that is topped with anything you can imagine — from vegetables and cheeses to meats and seafood, and drizzled with extra virgin olive oil right before serving. Later in this chapter, I provide a recipe (page 118) for a Roasted Yellow Pepper Bruschetta with Fresh Mozzarella that works well on the antipasto plate (in a smaller version). It's easy to create your own too. Some great combinations are chopped tomatoes with fresh basil and balsamic vinegar, Tapenade (recipe, page 166) with grilled seafood, fresh pecorino cheese with olives and walnuts or marinated artichokes with thinly sliced dry salami and Parmesan cheese.

CAPRESE: Layer a slice of fresh mozzarella cheese with a slice of ripe tomato, repeat for a second layer and add a few fresh basil leaves to complete the stack. Drizzle with extra virgin olive oil, balsamic vinegar, a few turns of freshly ground black pepper and a sprinkling of kosher salt.

*Wine Notes*

*Antipasto offers such a broad range of flavors and textures that it is best served with lighter, simpler and, therefore, more versatile wines. For a white, the light citrus and tangy acidity of a pinot grigio from Alto Adige cleanses the palate between bites. For a red, the light cherry and warm earthiness of a Montepulciano d'Abruzzo will playfully blend the flavors of the meats and cheeses.* ■

ROASTED PEPPERS WITH OLIVES AND PARMESAN CHEESE: Burn the skin of a bell pepper over an open flame and place in a plastic bag to steam for 3 minutes. Peel away the charred skin. Cut in half and remove the seeds and stem. Cut into large strips. Top with whole pitted olives, freshly shaved Parmesan cheese, a drizzle of extra virgin olive oil and a pinch of freshly ground black pepper and kosher salt.

MORTADELLA, PESTO AND MOZZARELLA WRAPS: Mortadella is an Italian sausage similar to the American bologna but with chunks of white fat and whole pistachios running through it. On our last trip to Italy we encountered a mortadella in one meat shop that weighed 105 kilograms (about 230 pounds) and measured 12 inches in diameter. That was one large cold cut. Lay a thin slice of mortadella on the counter and place an almond-sized piece of fresh mozzarella on the mortadella closest to you. Top with half a teaspoon of fresh Pesto (recipe, page 220 in my first cookbook) and wrap up into a tight bundle, folding the edges in. Sear the bundles on each side in a sauté pan with a little olive oil.

# CRISPY LOBSTER AND ASPARAGUS SPRING ROLLS WITH A GINGER-WASABI BUTTER

SERVES 4

ONE 1½ POUND LIVE MAINE LOBSTER
1 POUND LARGE ASPARAGUS SPEARS
8 SHEETS ROUND RICE PAPER
3 OUNCES ARUGULA
3 SCALLIONS, GREEN PART ONLY, SLICED THINLY
1 TABLESPOON FURIKAKE (JAPANESE BLEND OF SESAME SEEDS, NORI AND BONITO)
KOSHER SALT AND GROUND BLACK PEPPER TO TASTE
CANOLA OIL FOR FRYING

*These spring rolls combine some great Maine ingredients and add an Asian twist. Rice paper forms a crisp, textured casing around the moist lobster meat and the tender asparagus. Furikake is a Japanese condiment used to season rice. The traditional blend contains a mixture of sesame seeds, nori (seaweed) and bonito (dried and ground fish). Many variations of Furikake exist with other dried ingredients, ranging from flaked vegetables to eggs or salmon.* ■

THINLY SLICED SCALLIONS FOR GARNISH
GINGER-WASABI BUTTER SAUCE (RECIPE FOLLOWS)

*Wine Notes*

*The dominant flavors of asparagus, ginger and wasabi would overpower most wines, which is why riesling is the natural choice. Riesling's off-dry fruitiness and bracing acidity cuts through the heat of the ginger and wasabi flavors and softens the grassiness of the asparagus allowing the lobster to show through. Dr. L from Germany or Eroica from Washington State are fine matches.* ∎

1. Fill a large 9-quart stockpot with two inches of water; cover and bring to a boil. Add the live lobster, cover and cook for 10 minutes. Remove from the water and let cool. When cool, crack the lobster and remove the meat from the claws, knuckles and tail (discarding the vein and shells). Cut the claws and tail meat into ¼-inch-thick strips.

2. Cut the tough bottom part from the asparagus spears and peel the skin from the remaining bottom half. Blanch the asparagus spears in salted, boiling water for 2 minutes, and shock immediately in a bath of ice water. Once cooled, remove the asparagus from the water and dry. Cut the spears in half widthwise.

3. Place the rice paper sheets on a flat surface and brush with a little warm water. Let them sit for a few minutes to absorb the water and become pliable. If they are still hard in places, brush with a little more water.

4. Divide the lobster, asparagus, arugula and scallions between the 8 rounds of rice paper, placing a pile at the front of each sheet. Sprinkle with the Furikake, salt and black pepper. The tricky part of rolling these spring rolls is to roll them tightly without tearing the rice paper, so take your time. Starting with the front edge of the rice paper, roll it up over the filling and continue rolling it up ¾ of the way. Bring the sides in to enclose the filling and finish rolling it the rest of the way.

5. Allow the finished spring rolls to sit for at least 10 minutes before frying to allow the rice paper to form a seal. Fry in hot (375 degree) canola oil for 3 minutes, or until lightly browned. To achieve a crisp spring roll, it is necessary to flip them over while frying.

6. With a serrated knife, slice the spring rolls in half on a slight bias. Stack four halves in the center of each serving plate and surround with the ginger-wasabi butter sauce. Garnish with sliced scallions.

## GINGER-WASABI BUTTER SAUCE

1/3 CUP UNSALTED BUTTER
1 TABLESPOON CANOLA OIL
2 TABLESPOONS CHOPPED YELLOW ONION
1/2 CUP WHITE WINE
1 TABLESPOON PEELED AND MINCED FRESH GINGER
1/2 CUP HEAVY CREAM
1 TABLESPOON LIME JUICE
2 TABLESPOONS SWEET CHILI SAUCE
2 TEASPOONS WASABI PASTE
2 TEASPOONS COARSELY CHOPPED FRESH CILANTRO
2 TABLESPOONS SOY SAUCE (SHOYU)

1. Dice the butter and bring to room temperature.

2. Heat the oil in a small 2-quart saucepan. Sauté the onions over medium heat for 2 minutes but do not allow them to brown. Deglaze with the white wine, add the ginger and reduce over medium heat until most of the liquid has evaporated. Again, do not brown. Add the heavy cream and reduce the mixture by half, whisking occasionally.

3. Remove the pan from the heat and immediately whisk in the butter until well incorporated. Strain through a fine mesh strainer into a small bowl, discarding the solids. In a small bowl, combine and mix together the lime juice, sweet chili sauce, wasabi paste, cilantro and soy sauce. Stir this mixture into the butter sauce and keep in a warm place (not too hot or it will break) until serving.

*A mild French butter sauce clashes with pungent and aromatic Asian flavors to create this unique and delicious sauce. Whether you're serving with spring rolls, fried wontons or warm seafood, this sauce is truly outstanding and goes well with many Asian dishes. Wasabi (Japanese horseradish) has an extremely strong flavor and a small amount goes a long way. The amount of wasabi added to the sauce can be adjusted up or down, depending on personal taste. ■*

# Stilton Cheese and Shrimp Tartlet with Toasted Pine Nuts and Bosc Pears

SERVES 6

1 BATCH PASTRY DOUGH (RECIPE FOLLOWS)
VEGETABLE OIL
1 TABLESPOON UNSALTED BUTTER
12 LARGE SHRIMP, PEELED AND DEVEINED (16–20 PER POUND)
4 OUNCES CREAM CHEESE
5 OUNCES STILTON CHEESE
2 EGG YOLKS
2 TEASPOONS CHOPPED ITALIAN PARSLEY
3/4 CUP HEAVY CREAM
KOSHER SALT AND WHITE PEPPER TO TASTE
1 BATCH CHIVE BEURRE BLANC (RECIPE FOLLOWS)
1 RIPE BOSC PEAR (OTHER PEAR VARIETIES MAY BE USED)
2 TABLESPOONS PINE NUTS, TOASTED

1. Preheat the oven to 350 degrees.

2. Cut six 6-inch rounds of parchment paper. Roll out the dough on a lightly floured surface to ⅛ inch thick. Cut into six 5½-inch circles and form into 4-inch tartlet pans (with removable bottoms) that have been sprayed (or brushed) with vegetable oil. The dough should evenly coat the bottom and sides of the tartlet mold. Reserve the remaining dough for another use.

3. Place one 6-inch parchment round on top of each tartlet and fill with dry beans or pie weights. Bake in the preheated oven for 25 minutes. Remove the tartlets from the oven and empty out the beans or pie weights and parchment paper.

Shrimp and Stilton cheese are great together in this delectable appetizer. Other combinations that work well in their place are feta cheese and pitted Greek olives, cubed fresh mozzarella cheese with roasted pepper strips and shredded prosciutto, or pulled roasted chicken with herbed Boursin cheese. ■

Wine Notes

*With the richness of the cheese and delicate flavors of shrimp and pears, this dish needs a wine that has both weight and subtlety. The chenin blanc grape can provide both, with elegant pear and green apple flavors followed by a cool, creamy, lingering finish. Dry Creek Vineyards produces a lighter version while Moncontour Vouvray expands the flavors of the grape. ∎*

4. Heat a large sauté pan over medium-high heat. When the pan is hot, add the butter and cook the shrimp for 1 minute on each side, searing them but not cooking them through. Remove from the heat and onto a plate to stop the cooking. Season with salt and white pepper.

5. Combine the cream cheese and Stilton together in a mixing bowl and mix until smooth. Add the egg yolks, 1 teaspoon of the chopped parsley, the heavy cream and mix well. Season with salt and white pepper.

6. Divide the cheese mixture between the tart crusts and place two cooked shrimp on the top of each tartlet. Place the tartlets on a baking sheet and bake in the 350-degree oven for about 50 minutes.

7. To serve, halve, core and slice the pear into 18 thin wedges. Place the tart in the middle of the serving plate and surround with a few Tablespoons of the chive beurre blanc. Arrange three pear slices on each plate, leaning them against the tartlet, and sprinkle with the toasted pine nuts and the remaining chopped parsley.

## PASTRY DOUGH

1 1/3 CUPS ALL-PURPOSE FLOUR
3/4 TEASPOON KOSHER SALT
4 TABLESPOONS UNSALTED BUTTER, CHILLED
1/3 CUP VEGETABLE SHORTENING
1/4 CUP COLD WATER

1. In a mixer, combine the flour and salt. Cut the butter into fine cubes and mix into the flour until it resembles a fine meal. Add the shortening and mix for 30 seconds. Add the water and mix only until it combines. Do not overwork. Remove from the mixer and wrap in plastic wrap.

2. Refrigerate for at least 2 hours.

## CHIVE BEURRE BLANC

2 TABLESPOONS UNSALTED BUTTER
1½ TEASPOONS CANOLA OIL
½ SMALL YELLOW ONION, FINELY CHOPPED
¼ CUP WHITE WINE
1 TABLESPOON WHITE WINE VINEGAR
¼ CUP HEAVY CREAM
KOSHER SALT AND WHITE PEPPER TO TASTE
1 TABLESPOON FINELY CHOPPED CHIVES

1. Dice the butter and bring to room temperature.

2. Heat the oil in a small 2-quart saucepan. Sauté the onions over medium heat for 2 minutes, but do not allow them to brown. Deglaze with the white wine and vinegar and reduce over medium heat until most of the liquid has evaporated. Again, do not brown. Add the heavy cream and reduce the mixture by half, whisking occasionally.

3. Remove the pan from the heat and immediately whisk in the butter until well incorporated. Strain through a fine mesh strainer into a small bowl, discarding the solids. Season with salt and white pepper and stir in the chives. Keep in a warm place (not too hot or it will break) until serving.

# Zucchini-Wrapped Jumbo Shrimp with Soft Polenta and Mediterranean Olives

SERVES 4

12 LARGE (16–20 COUNT) SHRIMP, PEELED AND DEVEINED
2 TABLESPOONS EXTRA VIRGIN OLIVE OIL
1/4 TEASPOON KOSHER SALT
1/8 TEASPOON FRESHLY GROUND BLACK PEPPER
1 TEASPOON HERBES DE PROVENCE
2 MEDIUM-SIZED ZUCCHINI
2 TABLESPOONS MINCED GARLIC
1/4 CUP EXTRA VIRGIN OLIVE OIL
3/4 CUP COUNTRY MIXED OLIVES (VARIETY), PITTED
1/2 CUP THINLY SLICED ROASTED RED BELL PEPPERS
2 TABLESPOONS COARSELY CHOPPED ITALIAN PARSLEY
1 BATCH SOFT POLENTA (RECIPE FOLLOWS)
1 BATCH HONEY-SHALLOT VINAIGRETTE (RECIPE FOLLOWS)

1. Place the shrimp in a medium-sized bowl and add 1 Tablespoon olive oil, the salt, black pepper and herbes de Provence, and mix well to coat.

2. Remove the ends of the two zucchini. Using a mandoline, slice the zucchini lengthwise into long thin strips, getting some of the green outside on each slice and leaving the interior core. You need 12 nice slices for this recipe.

3. Place a zucchini slice on the work surface and lay a shrimp on top. Roll the zucchini tightly around the shrimp and secure the end with a toothpick. Continue with the remaining shrimp and place the wrapped shrimp on a plate. Using the bowl from the marinated shrimp (and any of the remaining

*Soave, the plonk wine*

*of the late 1960s, has been*

*reinvented by Stefano Inama.*

*His soave classico, with its*

*signature green apple and pear*

*aromas and light minerality,*

*dance through the more defined*

*flavors of the zucchini and*

*olives and bring forth the*

*sweet, simple quality of the*

*shrimp.* ∎

marinade), combine the remaining 1 Tablespoon of olive oil and 1 Tablespoon of the minced garlic. Drizzle over the wrapped shrimp.

4. Heat a grill pan (or outside BBQ grill) over high heat and preheat the oven to 400 degrees.

5. Heat the olive oil in a medium-sized sauté pan over medium heat. When hot, add the remaining Tablespoon of garlic and stir until lightly browned. Add the olives and roasted red bell pepper strips and heat through, about 3 minutes. Stir in the Italian parsley and remove to a bowl and keep warm.

6. When the grill pan is hot, grill the zucchini-wrapped shrimp on each side until well marked from the grill. Remove the shrimp to an ovenproof plate and finish cooking in the preheated oven for about 5 minutes.

7. To serve, place a scoop of the soft polenta in the center of each plate and arrange three shrimp evenly around the plate. Divide the olive mixture between the plates and drizzle each with the honey-shallot vinaigrette. Serve immediately.

## SOFT POLENTA

> 2 CUPS WATER
> 1/2 CUP YELLOW CORNMEAL
> 1/2 TEASPOON KOSHER SALT
> 2 TABLESPOONS UNSALTED BUTTER

1. Combine ½ cup of water with the cornmeal and salt.

2. Boil the remaining 1½ cups of water over high heat. At a boil, whisk the softened cornmeal into the water, stirring constantly until thickened. Cover and reduce the heat to low, continuing to cook for 5 minutes. Add the butter and stir until melted and combined.

## HONEY-SHALLOT VINAIGRETTE

1 SHALLOT, MINCED
1/2 TEASPOON DIJON MUSTARD
2 TABLESPOONS SHERRY WINE VINEGAR
2 TEASPOONS HONEY
1/3 CUP EXTRA VIRGIN OLIVE OIL
KOSHER SALT AND FRESHLY GROUND BLACK PEPPER TO TASTE
1 TEASPOON CHOPPED ITALIAN PARSLEY

1. Combine the minced shallot, Dijon mustard, sherry wine vinegar and honey in a small bowl and whisk together.

2. Slowly add the olive oil while whisking vigorously, until incorporated. Season with salt and pepper and stir in the parsley.

## DILL GNOCCHI WITH LOBSTER AND WILD MUSHROOMS

SERVES 4

TWO 1 1/2 POUND LIVE MAINE LOBSTERS
1 BATCH DILL GNOCCHI (RECIPE FOLLOWS)
2 TABLESPOONS EXTRA VIRGIN OLIVE OIL
2 CLOVES GARLIC, MINCED
1 POUND FRESH WILD MUSHROOMS (MORELS, PORCINI, OYSTER, TRUMPET, CHANTERELLES, ETC.), CLEANED
1 BAG BABY SPINACH (6 OUNCES)
KOSHER SALT AND CRACKED BLACK PEPPER
1/4 CUP DRY WHITE WINE
1/2 CUP BOTTLED CLAM JUICE
1 CUP HEAVY CREAM
2 TABLESPOONS CHOPPED FRESH DILL

*Fresh wild mushrooms are seasonal and their availability can be limited. If you can only find more common cultivated varieties like portabella and shiitake mushrooms, try adding some reconstituted dried mushrooms to the mix. Soak your dried mushrooms in warm water to cover for about 15 minutes to reconstitute. Chop the mushrooms and add as you would the fresh. Decant the soaking liquid, discarding any sand or grit at the bottom of the bowl and add the liquid with the clam juice for a more flavorful reduction.* ■

JUICE AND ZEST FROM 1/2 LEMON
PARMESAN CHEESE, FRESHLY GRATED
4 SPRIGS FRESH DILL FOR GARNISH

1. For the lobsters, fill a large (9-quart or larger) stockpot with 2 inches of water, cover and bring to a boil. Add the live lobsters, cover and cook for 10 minutes. Remove from the water and let cool. When cool, crack the lobsters and remove the meat from the claws, knuckles and tails (discarding the vein). Discard shells and reserve the lobster meat.

2. Bring a large pot of salted water to a boil to reheat the precooked dill gnocchi.

3. Rip the mushrooms into pieces about the size of a quarter. Place a large sauté pan over medium-high heat. When hot, add the olive oil and garlic and cook for 20 seconds while stirring. Stir in the mushrooms and cook for 1 minute, stirring. Add the cooked lobster meat and heat through. Add the baby spinach and season with salt and pepper. Stir and cook briefly, lightly wilting the spinach. Remove the mixture from the pan, cover and keep warm.

4. Return the pan to high heat and add the white wine and clam juice. Reduce until almost dry and add the heavy cream. Reduce the cream by half, resulting in a nice smooth cream sauce. Finish the sauce with the chopped dill, lemon juice and lemon zest. Season with salt and pepper to taste.

5. While the cream is reducing, drop the dill gnocchi in the boiling water and reheat for 2 minutes. Drain quickly and toss into the finished sauce. Divide the gnocchi between four serving bowls and top with the lobster-mushroom mixture.

6. Serve with freshly grated Parmesan cheese and a sprig of fresh dill.

## Wine Notes

*To stand up to the intense flavors of dill and wild mushrooms, a wine of dominant character is needed. Great Napa Valley chardonnay, with its clean citrus fruit, its vanilla and toasty oak mid-palate and soft creamy finish is the clear choice for this dish. Grgich Cellars and Trefethen Vineyards have long made excellent examples.* ▪

## Dill Gnocchi

2 LARGE BAKING IDAHO POTATOES (2 POUNDS)
1 EGG
2 TABLESPOONS MINCED FRESH DILL
2 TEASPOONS KOSHER SALT
1/4 TEASPOON GROUND WHITE PEPPER
PINCH FRESHLY GRATED NUTMEG
1 1/2 CUPS ALL-PURPOSE FLOUR (PLUS MORE FOR WORKING
    THE DOUGH)
1/4 CUP FRESHLY GRATED PARMESAN CHEESE

*Gnocchi (Italian for dumplings) are fun to make and students in my cooking classes are usually quite amazed with how easy they can be to produce. I use a fork in this recipe to make the ridges on the back of the gnocchi, which works fine. A gnocchi board is a ribbed wooden board specifically designed for making the ridges on the back of gnocchi. This unique tool makes the process much quicker and forms more uniform dumplings.* ■

1. Place the cleaned potatoes in a large saucepan and cover with cold water. Bring the water to a boil and reduce to a simmer, cooking the potatoes for about 30 minutes after the boil has been reached.

2. Using a kitchen towel to hold the potatoes, peel them with a paring knife while they are still hot. Press them through a potato ricer onto a clean counter and gently spread them out to cool.

3. Crack the egg into a small bowl and whisk together with the dill, salt, white pepper and nutmeg.

4. Mound the cooled potatoes on the counter and pour the beaten egg mixture into a well in the center. Mix the egg slowly into the potatoes and start adding the flour and Parmesan cheese in batches, kneading the mixture into a dough. Knead the dough for 2 minutes.

5. Cut the dough into 8 pieces. Take each piece of dough and roll it into a rope about 1/2 inch thick. Use flour if necessary to prevent the dough from sticking and slice the rope into 1/2-inch pieces.

6. To form the gnocchi shape: If you're right-handed, hold a dinner fork (facing up) in your left hand with the tines resting on the counter at a 45-degree

angle. Flour your left thumb, start the piece of dough at the top of the tines and gently press the dough into the tines as you roll it down to the base of the tines. As the dough rolls down, allow it to form around your thumb, creating the indentation on the smooth side while the other side forms ribs from the tines of the fork.

7. Place the gnocchi on a floured parchment-lined baking sheet and continue forming gnocchi with all of the dough.

8. Cooking the gnocchi: After being formed, the gnocchi need to be cooked immediately in a large pot of boiling salted water. Cook in two batches unless you have an enormous pot. Drop the gnocchi into the boiling water a few at a time, stirring continuously. When the gnocchi begin to float on the surface, cook them for 1 more minute and remove them to a lightly oiled baking sheet to cool in a single layer.

## BAKED ARTICHOKE WITH MAINE LOBSTER AND A YOGURT-FETA CHEESE DIP

SERVES 4

4 LARGE ARTICHOKES
1/2 LEMON
TWO 1 1/2 POUND LIVE MAINE LOBSTERS
3 TABLESPOONS EXTRA VIRGIN OLIVE OIL
KOSHER SALT AND FRESHLY GROUND BLACK PEPPER TO TASTE
4 TABLESPOONS UNSALTED BUTTER, SOFT
1/4 CUP FETA CHEESE, COARSELY CRUMBLED
1 TABLESPOON CHOPPED FLAT LEAF PARSLEY
1/2 CUP BREAD CRUMBS
YOGURT-FETA CHEESE DIP (RECIPE FOLLOWS)

*Eating artichokes is a task in and of itself. To begin with, the outer leaves are pulled out of the artichoke and the inner basal part is dipped into the Yogurt-Feta Cheese Dip. This dipped lower part of the leaf is eaten by pulling it off between your teeth. The leaf is discarded and this continues until all the leaves are gone. The bottom is then left with the lobster filling and can be eaten in its entirety because the choke has been removed.* ■

116 ■ HARTSTONE INN

1. Bring 1 gallon of water to a boil in a large stockpot set over high heat. To prepare the artichokes, cut the top third off the artichokes with a large sharp knife. Cut off the very tip from the stem, peel the outside layer from the stem and remove the first two layers of small leaves from the bottom of the artichoke with a paring knife. Place the artichokes in the boiling water and squeeze the half lemon into the pot. Carefully balance a plate over the artichokes to submerge them in the water. Cook the artichokes for 15 minutes, remove to a plate and cool.

2. Bring the water back to a boil, add the lobsters to the pot and cover. Cook the lobsters for 6 minutes and remove to a baking sheet to cool.

3. When the artichokes are cooled slightly, remove the small inner leaves, exposing the choke. The choke is the hair-like fibers growing from the inside bottom of the artichoke. With a teaspoon, gently scrape the fibers of the choke, exposing the smooth bottom. Remove the entire choke and discard.

4. Place the artichokes in a 9 x 12-inch baking pan with high sides and drizzle the inside of each artichoke with olive oil and sprinkle with salt and black pepper, getting between the leaves as well as in the cavity where the choke was.

5. Preheat the oven to 350 degrees.

6. When the lobsters are cool, crack and remove the meat from the claws, knuckles and tails (discarding the vein). Discard the shells and cut the lobster meat into 1-inch pieces. Place the lobster meat in a small bowl and toss with the soft butter, crumbled feta and most of the parsley. Season with salt and pepper.

7. Divide the lobster mixture between the cavities of the four artichokes. Sprinkle each artichoke with bread crumbs, getting some in between the leaves, and sprinkle with the remaining parsley.

8. Place the artichokes in the preheated oven and bake for 35 minutes. Serve immediately with a healthy portion of the yogurt-feta cheese dip.

*Wine Notes*

*Artichokes are one of the toughest food pairings. Its distinctive flavors call for a wine with its own unique qualities. White Rhone wines, which can be a blend of up to eight grape varieties, including viognier, marsanne and roussane, provide incredible floral aromatics along with hints of earth and spice. This will temper the intensity of the artichoke and bring forth the flavors of lobster and cheese. Guigal Cotes du Rhone Blanc is a fine example.* ■

## Yogurt-Feta Cheese Dip

2 CUPS PLAIN YOGURT
1/2 CUP FINELY CRUMBLED FETA CHEESE
2 TABLESPOONS OLIVE OIL
1/2 TEASPOON MINCED GARLIC
1/2 LEMON, JUICE AND MINCED ZEST
2 PINCHES CAYENNE PEPPER
2 PINCHES KOSHER SALT
1 PINCH WHITE PEPPER

1. Place the yogurt in a very fine mesh strainer set over a deep container. Quite a bit of the whey will drain from the yogurt, so make sure the strainer is set up high enough to collect the whey without resting in it. Cover the yogurt with plastic wrap and refrigerate for 12 hours.

2. Place the drained yogurt in a bowl (discarding the whey) and add the remaining ingredients. Mix well.

## Roasted Yellow Pepper Bruschetta with Fresh Mozzarella

SERVES 4

4 TABLESPOONS EXTRA VIRGIN OLIVE OIL
1/2 CUP FINELY CHOPPED YELLOW ONION
2 TABLESPOONS BALSAMIC VINEGAR
10 LARGE BASIL LEAVES
KOSHER SALT AND FRESHLY GROUND BLACK PEPPER
1 LARGE YELLOW BELL PEPPER
4 HALF-INCH-THICK SLICES OF CRUSTY COUNTRY-STYLE BREAD
   (APPROX. SIZE: 5 X 2 INCHES)
2 WHOLE PEELED CLOVES OF GARLIC

*Canned or bottled roasted peppers can't hold a candle to those roasted over an open flame either in your own kitchen or on a barbecue grill. Any color of ripe bell pepper will work well and a combination of colors is nice too. If buffalo milk mozzarella is available, try it for a more authentic Italian flavor.* ■

2 LARGE (4 OUNCES) BALLS OF FRESH MOZZARELLA
EXTRA VIRGIN OLIVE OIL TO DRIZZLE

1. Heat a medium-sized sauté pan over medium-high heat. Add 1 Tablespoon of the olive oil and then the chopped onions. Cook the onions for about 10 minutes, or until they are well caramelized, stirring occasionally. Deglaze the pan with the balsamic vinegar and reduce for about 5 minutes, or until the vinegar becomes a glaze. Remove to a small bowl and let cool. When cool, stir in 1 Tablespoon of olive oil, 4 basil leaves that have been finely chopped and season with salt and freshly ground black pepper.

2. Burn the skin of the bell pepper over an open flame and place in a plastic bag to steam for 3 minutes. Peel away the charred skin. Cut in half and remove the seeds and stem. Cut into 8 strips.

3. Heat a grill pan over high heat. Brush both sides of the bread slices with the remaining 2 Tablespoons of olive oil and grill in the hot pan, making nice golden brown grill marks on each side of the bread.

4. Remove the bread from the pan and rub each slice with the whole garlic cloves, like you would use a grater. The garlic will "grate" into the bread.

5. Slice each mozzarella ball into 6 slices and finely slice 2 of the remaining basil leaves.

6. Spread the onion mixture evenly onto the grilled bread slices, and top with alternating slices of fresh mozzarella and roasted peppers. Sprinkle the top with the finely sliced basil and the final garnish of a whole basil leaf. Place on a serving platter and drizzle the entire platter with extra virgin olive oil.

## Wine Notes

*In Italy's Veneto region, valpolicella is served slightly chilled during the warmer months. This red wine's delicate cherry fruit and whispers of exotic spices will perfectly complement the slightly herbal quality of the peppers and the subtle richness of the cheese. Roberto Mazzi makes one of the best examples at any temperature.* ■

# Beet Ravioli with a Pine Nut Butter Sauce

### SERVES 6

## BEET FILLING

2 LARGE RED BEETS (1 POUND)
1/4 CUP WHOLE MILK RICOTTA CHEESE
2 TABLESPOONS GRATED PARMESAN CHEESE
1 TABLESPOON BREAD CRUMBS
KOSHER SALT AND WHITE PEPPER TO TASTE

1. Wrap the beets in aluminum foil and place in a preheated 400-degree oven and roast for about 1 hour. Carefully remove the foil and allow the beets to cool.

2. Once cool enough to handle, peel the beets by gently pushing with your fingers. Discard the peel. Cut one beet into batonnets (thick sticks ½ x ½ x 2 inches) and reserve. Using a hand grater, grate the other beet finely into a medium-sized bowl. Add the remaining ingredients to the grated beet and mix well. Adjust the seasoning with salt and white pepper.

## EGG PASTA DOUGH

1¼ CUPS PASTA FLOUR (SEMOLINA)
1 LARGE EGG, SLIGHTLY BEATEN
1/2 TEASPOON KOSHER SALT
1½ TEASPOONS EXTRA VIRGIN OLIVE OIL
2 TABLESPOONS WARM WATER

1. Place the flour on a clean working counter and make a well in the center. Add the remaining ingredients to the center of the well and gradually mix the dry

My first cookbook has a whole section on making, forming and cooking pasta, and some terrific recipes for fresh sauces to use with the fresh pasta. Since I was a little boy, I have loved the flavor and texture of beets and this simple recipe really showcases those qualities. ∎

ingredients into the wet, forming a smooth, soft dough (adding additional water if necessary to make the dough soft).

2. Knead the dough 10 minutes, wrap tightly with plastic wrap and refrigerate for 1 hour. *This recipe makes about a $^1/_2$ pound of dough.*

## ROLLING OUT THE DOUGH AND SHAPING THE RAVIOLI

1. Once your pasta has set up for at least 1 hour in the refrigerator, remove it from the plastic and press it down into a disk on a floured (semolina) work surface. Cut the dough into 2 equal pieces and rewrap the second piece in the plastic wrap to prevent it from drying out.

2. With a rolling pin and extra semolina (if needed), roll the dough out to about ¼ inch thick. If the dough seems sticky, dust it with some semolina.

3. Set up the pasta machine with a setting of 1 (the highest, thickest setting) and roll the pasta through. Again, if the dough seems sticky, dust it with some semolina. Adjust the thickness to 6 and run the dough through the machine at that setting.

4. Lay the dough out on a floured (semolina) work surface and use a 3½-inch-round scalloped cutter to cut out as many rounds as you can. Have a small bowl available with about half a cup of warm water in it. Wet your index fingertip in the bowl and gently brush the outside circumference of the circle.

5. Place 1 Tablespoon of the beet filling in the center of the circle that is wet and place another circle on top of the filling. Work your way around the ravioli, patting the two circles together to work out any air pockets.

6. Place the completed ravioli in a single layer on a baking sheet dusted with

semolina. Repeat Step 5 until you finish making the remaining ravioli. For an appetizer portion, 3 raviolis per person will be sufficient. The remaining raviolis can be kept fresh for a few days or frozen. *I normally place the entire baking sheet in the freezer to allow the raviolis to freeze individually and then transfer them to freezer bags to be stored for up to 3 months.*

7. Working in batches, cook the ravioli in a pot of boiling salted water until tender, about 3 minutes if fresh, or 7 to 9 minutes if frozen. Drain well.

## PINE NUT BUTTER SAUCE

> 2 TABLESPOONS UNSALTED BUTTER
> 2 TABLESPOONS CRUSHED PINE NUTS
> FRESHLY GROUND BLACK PEPPER
> 1 TABLESPOON MINCED ITALIAN PARSLEY
> 1/4 CUP SHAVED PARMESAN CHEESE
> 2 TABLESPOONS WHOLE TOASTED PINE NUTS FOR GARNISH
> 6 GRILLED TIGER SHRIMP (OPTIONAL)

1. Place the butter in a medium-sized sauté pan and place over medium-high heat. Allow the butter to brown slightly.

2. Add the crushed pine nuts, a few grinds of black pepper and the cooked ravioli. Heat through and toss in the Italian parsley. Season with kosher salt if necessary.

3. In a small sauté pan, heat the batonnets of beets up in a little butter and season with salt and black pepper. Transfer the raviolis to plates, drizzling any remaining sauce from the pan over the ravioli. Divide the beet batonnets among the plates and sprinkle with the shaved Parmesan and whole pine nuts, topping with a grilled shrimp (if desired).

*Pine nuts (pignoli in Italian) are the edible seeds of certain types of pine trees. In the U.S., we harvest the nuts from various species of pinyon pine trees while in Europe the nut comes from Stone pine trees. In this dish, the pine nuts play a minor role of texture and flavor when matched with the bold taste of fresh beets in the ravioli. ∎*

Soups & Salads

# Baby Spinach with Cumin-Roasted Pear and Maytag Blue Cheese

SERVES 6

3 BOSC PEARS
3 TABLESPOONS WALNUT OIL
2 TABLESPOONS PORT WINE
2 TABLESPOONS LIGHT BROWN SUGAR, FIRMLY PACKED
1/4 TEASPOON KOSHER SALT
2 TABLESPOONS CUMIN SPICE MIX (RECIPE FOLLOWS)
1/3 CUP WALNUT HALVES
1/3 CUP DRIED CRANBERRIES
10 OUNCES BABY SPINACH
HONEY AND WALNUT DRESSING (RECIPE FOLLOWS)
1/4 POUND MAYTAG BLUE CHEESE (OR OTHER GOOD QUALITY
    CREAMY BLUE CHEESE), CRUMBLED

1. Preheat the oven to 400 degrees.

2. Peel the pears and cut in half lengthwise. Remove the core and stem with a melon baller and cut each half into 3 equal wedges.

3. In a medium-sized bowl, whisk together the walnut oil, port wine, brown sugar, salt and cumin spice mix. Add the pear wedges, walnut halves and dried cranberries and toss to evenly coat.

4. Place a Silpat mat or piece of parchment paper on a baking sheet and spread out the pear mixture on top. Roast in the preheated oven for 10 minutes. Remove and cool to room temperature.

5. To serve, toss the baby spinach with enough of the honey and walnut dressing

The honey and walnut dressing in this recipe is so flavorful and versatile it has become a staple in my kitchen. I use it in many appetizers and salad dishes I serve in the restaurant, changing the type of nuts and nut oils used, depending on the dish. A nice fall recipe I prepare starts with cooked and peeled beets, which are thinly sliced, served with roasted duckling and topped with the dressing. ■

to coat. Arrange the baby spinach on the plate with the roasted pear wedges, cranberries, walnuts and crumbled blue cheese.

## CUMIN SPICE MIX

> 1/2 CUP LIGHT BROWN SUGAR, FIRMLY PACKED
> 2 TABLESPOONS CHILI POWDER
> 1 1/2 TEASPOONS GROUND CUMIN
> 2 TEASPOONS WHOLE CUMIN
> 1 TEASPOON GROUND CORIANDER
> 1/2 TEASPOON GROUND CARDAMOM
> 1/4 TEASPOON GROUND CINNAMON
> 1/4 TEASPOON GROUND CAYENNE PEPPER
> 2 TEASPOONS WHOLE ANISE SEEDS

1. Mix the sugar and spices together.

## HONEY AND WALNUT DRESSING

> 1/2 CUP WALNUT OIL
> 1 TABLESPOON CRUSHED WALNUTS
> 1 TABLESPOON MINCED SHALLOT
> 2 TABLESPOONS SHERRY VINEGAR
> 2 TEASPOONS DIJON MUSTARD
> 2 TABLESPOONS HONEY
> KOSHER SALT AND FRESHLY GROUND BLACK PEPPER

1. Heat the walnut oil in a small saucepan over medium heat. When it gets very warm (not hot), add the crushed walnuts and shallots and allow it to steep off the heat until cool.

2. In a medium-sized bowl, whisk together the vinegar, mustard and honey. While whisking, slowly drizzle in the cooled walnut oil until incorporated. Season with salt and pepper to taste.

*Wine Notes*

*The Maytag blue can easily stand up to a red wine but the more exotic cumin spice calls for a well-structured riesling from Germany's Reingau region. August Kesseler Estate riesling has a dominant ripe pear character with an almost electric acidity that will greatly enhance the spice and fruit components of this dish.* ◼

# ROASTED FENNEL AND YUKON GOLD POTATO SOUP

SERVES 6

2 LARGE HEADS FRESH FENNEL, RESERVING THE FRONDS
5 TABLESPOONS EXTRA VIRGIN OLIVE OIL
1 TEASPOON GROUND FENNEL SEED
KOSHER SALT AND BLACK PEPPER TO TASTE
1 MEDIUM ONION, CHOPPED
1/2 POUND YUKON GOLD POTATOES, PEELED AND DICED
1 QUART CHICKEN STOCK
1 SMALL BAY LEAF
1 TEASPOON LEMON JUICE
1 CUP HEAVY CREAM
1 TABLESPOON WHOLE FENNEL SEEDS
1/8 CUP GRATED PARMESAN CHEESE
1/8 CUP GRATED GRUYÈRE CHEESE

1. Preheat the oven to 350 degrees.

2. Slice the heads of fennel in half and remove the core. Cut off any fronds and reserve for garnish. Slice the fennel into ¼-inch-thick slices and lay on a cookie sheet lined with foil. Drizzle 1 Tablespoon of the olive oil over the fennel and season with the ground fennel seed, salt and pepper.

3. Roast the fennel in the preheated oven for 30 minutes.

4. Heat a medium-sized saucepan over medium-high heat. Add 2 Tablespoons olive oil and then the onions. Cook for 2 minutes, stirring occasionally. Add the potatoes and continue cooking for 5 minutes. Add the chicken stock and the bay leaf. Bring to a boil and reduce to a simmer for 20 minutes.

## Wine Notes

*Since fennel has the unique ability to make almost any red wine taste vegetal, white wine is definitely the choice. In this case, the slightly sweet and spicy qualities of a good gewurtztraminer will bring out the finer qualities of the fennel and complement the richness of the Yukon golds. The European versions from Sipp Mack in Alsace or Villa Wolf in Germany will provide the desired qualities without the overpowering sweetness of some New World offerings.* ■

5. Coarsely chop the roasted fennel, reserving six nice slices for garnish. Remove the bay leaf from the soup and add the chopped fennel, lemon juice and heavy cream. Cook for 10 more minutes.

6. Heat the remaining 2 Tablespoons of olive oil in a small sauté pan over medium heat. Add the whole fennel seeds and cook for 5 minutes. Strain off the seeds and reserve the fennel oil.

7. Puree the soup with either an immersion blender or a regular household blender until smooth. Return the soup to the pan and place over medium heat. Stir in the cheese and adjust the seasoning with salt.

8. Ladle the soup into the desired serving bowls. Garnish with the reserved slices of roasted fennel and the fennel fronds. Drizzle with the fennel oil and serve.

## Seafood Panzanella Salad

SERVES 6

2 POUNDS SEAFOOD OF YOUR CHOICE (LOBSTER, CRAB, SHRIMP, MUSSELS, TUNA, ETC.)
2 TEASPOONS FRESH LEMON JUICE
1 TABLESPOON CHOPPED ITALIAN PARSLEY
1/4 CUP, PLUS 2 TABLESPOONS EXTRA VIRGIN OLIVE OIL
2 TABLESPOONS BALSAMIC VINEGAR
KOSHER SALT AND FRESHLY GROUND BLACK PEPPER
3 RIPE TOMATOES, CORED AND COARSELY CHOPPED
1/2 CUP THINLY SLICED YELLOW ONION
2 CUPS CUBED BREAD (USE RUSTIC COUNTRY-STYLE BREAD WITHOUT THE CRUST AND CUT INTO 1/2-INCH CUBES)
1 CUP FRESH BASIL LEAVES
6 BASIL SPRIGS FOR GARNISH

1. Clean and cook the seafood using any method you desire. You can grill, poach, steam or sauté the seafood; just be careful to not overcook it. The other option is to buy seafood that is already cooked for you like crabmeat and shrimp to simplify this recipe.

2. Once you have your 2 pounds of seafood, free of shell and bones, cut any large pieces (like a whole lobster tail) into more manageable pieces. Drizzle the seafood with the lemon juice, the parsley, 2 Tablespoons olive oil and season with salt and black pepper to taste. Toss gently to coat and refrigerate until serving.

3. Make the balsamic vinaigrette by whisking together the remaining olive oil, the balsamic vinegar and season with salt and pepper to taste.

4. Core the tomatoes and cut into ½-inch wedges. Cut the wedges in half to create uniform chunks of tomatoes and mix together with the sliced onion and cubed bread. Tear the basil into small pieces and add to the tomato mixture along with the vinaigrette. Toss well to coat.

5. To serve, make a small ring of the tomato mixture on each plate and fill the center with the seafood. Garnish with the basil sprig and serve.

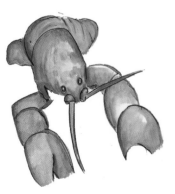

# Sweet Potato and Seafood Chowder with Asparagus

SERVES 6

2 Tablespoons unsalted butter
1 cup chopped yellow onion
1 pound sweet potatoes, peeled
3 cups fish stock (or bottled clam juice)
1 pound Yukon gold potatoes, cut into 1/2-inch dice
1/2 cup finely chopped celery
1/2 pound Maine sea scallops
1/4 pound Maine shrimp
1/2 cup chopped asparagus (discard tough stems)
1/2 cup heavy cream
1/2 pound Maine crabmeat
1 teaspoon chopped fresh dill
Kosher salt and white pepper to taste
4 slices Smoked Salmon and Asparagus Butter
   (recipe follows)

1. Place a large saucepan over medium-high heat and melt the butter. Add the chopped onions and cook, stirring, for 5 minutes, until the onions become translucent.

2. Cut the sweet potatoes into 1/2-inch pieces and add to the pan and continue cooking for 3 more minutes, stirring frequently.

3. Add the fish stock along with 2½ cups water. Bring the mixture to a boil, reduce to a simmer and cook for 25 minutes.

*Seafood chowders are really popular up here in New England and you will find them made with everything from clams and lobster to haddock and scallops. I use a combination of shrimp, scallops and crabmeat in this chowder recipe, but any type of seafood can be used, depending on availability and personal likes and dislikes. Seasonal vegetable supplements can bring out the best in your chowders: asparagus in the spring, corn in the summer and squash in the fall.* ■

Albarino is the white wine

of Spain's seacoast. The

delicate apricot fruit of the

wine balances the slight brown

sugar quality of the soup's

potatoes, while the crisp acidity

stands up to the sharpness of

the asparagus and the wine's

mystical aroma of ocean air

brings forth the fresh qualities

of the seafood. ■

4. Puree the soup with either an immersion blender or a regular household blender until smooth and return it to the pan. Add the diced potatoes and return to a simmer for 15 minutes over medium heat.

5. Add the celery, scallops, shrimp and asparagus to the pan and cook for 5 minutes.

6. Add the cream, crabmeat and dill and adjust the seasoning with salt and white pepper.

7. Ladle the soup into the desired serving bowls and top with a slice of the smoked salmon and asparagus butter.

### SMOKED SALMON AND ASPARAGUS BUTTER

4 LARGE SPEARS OF ASPARAGUS
1 OUNCE SMOKED SALMON
1/4 CUP (4 TABLESPOONS) UNSALTED BUTTER, SOFT
1 TEASPOON CHOPPED FRESH DILL
2 PINCHES KOSHER SALT
1 PINCH WHITE PEPPER

1. Cut the tough part (pale color) off the bottom of the asparagus spears and peel the lower half of the spears, removing the tougher outside shell. Blanch the asparagus in boiling water for 2 minutes to partially cook them and cool them off in a bowl of ice water. Dry them.

2. Place the dry asparagus in the bowl of a food processor and pulse until finely chopped. Add the smoked salmon and process again until a smooth paste forms.

3. Add the remaining ingredients and process gently until just combined.

4. Spoon the butter out onto parchment paper, forming a thick 1½-inch log. Roll into a smooth log and set up in the refrigerator for 30 minutes.

# Tossed Lobster Salad with an Anchovy-Chive Dressing

SERVES 6

THREE 1¼ POUND LIVE MAINE LOBSTERS
12 OUNCES ROMAINE HEARTS, CLEANED
1 ENGLISH (SEEDLESS) CUCUMBER
2 HAAS AVOCADOS
½ CUP ANCHOVY-CHIVE DRESSING (RECIPE FOLLOWS)
1 PINT GRAPE OR CHERRY TOMATOES
¼ CUP SHELLED SUNFLOWER SEEDS
12 WHOLE ANCHOVIES (OPTIONAL)

1. Fill a large 9-quart stockpot with two inches of water; cover and bring to a boil. Add the live lobsters, cover and cook for 12 minutes. Remove from the water and let cool. When cool, crack the lobster and remove the meat from the claws, knuckles and tail (discarding the vein and shells). Cut the claws and tail meat into ½-inch pieces and reserve.

2. Tear the romaine hearts into 1-inch pieces and place them in a large bowl. Cut the cucumber into ½-inch pieces and add to the bowl with the romaine.

3. Cut the avocados in half and remove the pit. Peel the skin from the avocado and cut the flesh into 1-inch pieces and reserve.

4. Add the dressing and cooked lobster meat to the bowl and toss with the romaine and cucumber.

5. Divide the salad between 6 bowls and top with the avocado, cherry tomatoes and sunflower seeds. Top with the optional anchovies if you wish.

*My tossed lobster salad is my take on the traditional Caesar salad, with a few of my favorite embellishments. The dressing can be made up to a week in advance, and if you can't get your hands on fresh lobsters, try shrimp or other seafood of your choice. Slice a warm French baguette and pour a glass of Champagne and you have a perfect summer lunch.* ■

## Anchovy-Chive Dressing

3 TEASPOONS MINCED GARLIC (ABOUT 6 CLOVES)
4 ANCHOVIES, CHOPPED
3 EGG YOLKS
1 LEMON, JUICED
1 1/2 CUPS EXTRA VIRGIN OLIVE OIL
1/2 TEASPOON KOSHER SALT
1/4 TEASPOON FRESHLY GROUND BLACK PEPPER
6 TABLESPOONS GRATED PARMESAN CHEESE
2 TABLESPOONS FINELY CHOPPED CHIVES

1. Combine the minced garlic, anchovies, egg yolks and lemon juice in the bowl of a food processor. Blend until combined.

2. With the food processor running, slowly drizzle in the olive oil until combined. Add the remaining ingredients and blend just until combined.

3. Keep chilled until ready to use.

# Roasted Sweet Potato, Rutabaga and Green Apple Soup

SERVES 6

1 LARGE SWEET POTATO
1 TABLESPOON OLIVE OIL
1/2 CUP (8 TABLESPOONS) UNSALTED BUTTER
1 CUP CHOPPED YELLOW ONIONS
1 CUP PEELED, DICED RUTABAGA
1 GRANNY SMITH APPLE, PEELED, CORED AND DICED
1 QUART CHICKEN STOCK
1 CUP HEAVY CREAM

Wine Notes

The anchovies will add a slight saltiness to this dish, which means a certain effervescence is required. An extra-dry Champagne (which is actually less dry than brut) will offer the needed sparkle, pleasant citrus fruit and crisp acidity necessary for this salad. ∎

1½ TABLESPOONS MAINE MAPLE SYRUP
KOSHER SALT AND WHITE PEPPER TO TASTE
MAPLE CREAM (RECIPE FOLLOWS)
¼ CUP CROUTONS
1 TABLESPOON SLICED SCALLIONS

1. Preheat the oven to 400 degrees.

2. Peel the sweet potato, slice into ½-inch-thick slices and lay on a foil-lined baking sheet. Drizzle with the olive oil and season with kosher salt and white pepper. Roast in the preheated oven for 30 minutes.

3. Place the butter in a large saucepan and place over medium heat. When the butter melts, add the onions and sweat for 3 minutes, stirring occasionally. Add the rutabaga and Granny Smith apple and continue to cook for 3 minutes, stirring occasionally. Add the chicken stock and the roasted sweet potatoes and simmer for 20 minutes.

4. Remove from the heat and blend the soup with either a handheld immersion blender or in a regular household blender until smooth. Add the cream, maple syrup and season with salt and white pepper. Bring back to a simmer and serve with a dollop of whipped maple cream, croutons and finely sliced scallions.

## MAPLE CREAM

⅓ CUP HEAVY CREAM
1 TABLESPOON PURE MAINE MAPLE SYRUP
SMALL PINCH OF WHITE PEPPER
LARGE PINCH OF KOSHER SALT

1. Place the heavy cream in a cold mixing bowl and whisk on high speed until stiff. Add the maple syrup, salt and white pepper and whisk to combine.

## Wine Notes

*Rich soups are one of the staples in the cooler climates where pinot blanc, or pinot bianco as it is known in Italy, is typically grown. This cousin to the pinot grigio grape has a distinctive green apple fruit and an intriguing blend of both creaminess and acidity. At its best (Trimbach from Alsace or St. Michael Eppan from Italy), it will have the body and depth to complement the bold flavors of this soup. ■*

# Portabella Mushroom Soup with a Sherry Cream

SERVES 6

1 TABLESPOON CANOLA OIL
1 CUP FINELY CHOPPED YELLOW ONION
1 POUND PORTABELLA MUSHROOMS, SLICED
1/4 CUP ALL-PURPOSE FLOUR
1/2 CUP DRY SHERRY
1/2 CUP DRY WHITE WINE
3 1/2 CUPS CHICKEN STOCK
1 SMALL BAY LEAF
KOSHER SALT AND WHITE PEPPER TO TASTE
SHERRY CREAM (RECIPE FOLLOWS)
CROUTONS AND COARSELY CHOPPED ITALIAN PARSLEY
   FOR GARNISH

1. Heat the canola oil in a 4-quart saucepan over medium-high heat. Add the onions and sweat for 3 minutes, stirring occasionally. Add the sliced portabella mushrooms and cook for 6 minutes, stirring occasionally, as the mushrooms begin to release their juice.

2. Stir in the flour and stir continually for 2 minutes. Add the dry sherry and white wine and cook for 2 minutes, using the spoon to release the flour mixture from the bottom of the pan. Add the chicken stock and bay leaf and bring the soup to a boil. Reduce the heat to a simmer and cook for 25 minutes, stirring occasionally.

3. Remove the bay leaf from the soup and puree the soup with either an immersion blender or a regular household blender until smooth and return

*Hands down, I have received more requests for this recipe than any other. Every fall, I supplement the portabellas with wild mushrooms I receive from my "mushroom guy," foraged from local woodlands.* ▪

it to the pan. Season with salt and white pepper and serve in a bowl with a dollop of the sherry cream, some croutons and coarsely chopped Italian parsley.

### SHERRY CREAM

$^1/_3$ CUP HEAVY CREAM
1 TEASPOON DRY SHERRY
SMALL PINCH OF WHITE PEPPER
LARGE PINCH OF KOSHER SALT

1. Place the heavy cream in a cold mixing bowl and whisk on high speed until stiff. Add the sherry, salt and white pepper and whisk to combine.

*H*

## Wine Notes

*Sherry has long been relegated to an ingredient, but it is first and foremost a wine. Good sherry shows a range of flavors from apricots and stone fruit to roasted nuts and caramel. In this case, a Vox Oloroso sherry, which is slightly off-dry, will blend beautifully with the earthy quality of the mushrooms and creaminess of the soup. Ivison and Emilio Lustau produce high quality, reasonably priced sherry.* ■

# Swoosh

Snowball Express, Exit Strategy, Slick and Slicker, Grateful Sled are just a few of the names of past amateur teams competing at the U.S. National Toboggan Championships held at the Camden Snow Bowl. Downhill skiing, 10 runs from beginner to expert, reigns as a winter sport there, but every February, no matter the weather, several hundred teams from across the United States and the United Kingdom polish up their wooden toboggans and show up with one desire — to race down the 400-foot-long wooden toboggan chute, the only one in the entire state of Maine.

Teams, comprised of all ages, from young kids to those in their seventies, and dressed as chickens, hot dogs, aliens and predators, you name it, compete in the 2-, 3- and 4-person toboggan races. Only 300 racing slots are available, and each year, they fill up quickly for this three-day event. Most teams compete for the fastest times, but a few pride themselves on coming in absolutely last in their division.

Camden Snow Bowl is located on an eastern slope of Ragged Mountain and faces Penobscot Bay. Originally built in 1935, in a stand of birch, the wooden toboggan chute has been rebuilt twice. The last time was in 1990, and the next year, the U.S. National Toboggan Championships came to be. This family-oriented costume party has become an event that draws people from all over to watch and to compete.

Pancake breakfasts are served each morning before the day's races begin. The qualifier heats are held on Saturday, and Saturday evening is the great Chili and Chowder Cook-Off. The toboggan chute finals and the Awards ceremonies and drawings take place on Sunday.

Depending on how fast one's toboggan is and the condition of the iced chute, competitors can scream down this track in under 9 seconds, averaging 40 to 50 miles an hour. It's a source of pride that they don't ride their brakes on this 70-foot drop from top to bottom, and at the bottom, they usually fishtail across more ice until they manage to come to a stop. What a major adrenaline rush for everybody, competitors and lookers-on alike.

Dress warmly (there's no rule that spectators can't wear costumes too) for this jubilant and raucous event. Come prepared to cheer somebody on, preferably with cowbells or a megaphone or simply a great set of lungs. ◾

Artist: Ryan
Canvas Size: 30x40
Price $1450

*Entrées*

# Phyllo-Wrapped Double Lamb Chops with a Rosemary-Mustard Aioli

SERVES 4

2 RACK OF LAMB, FRENCHED (WITH 8 RIB BONES)
5 TABLESPOONS EXTRA VIRGIN OLIVE OIL
KOSHER SALT AND BLACK PEPPER TO TASTE
1/2 CUP CRUMBLED FETA CHEESE
1/4 CUP CHOPPED SUN-DRIED TOMATOES
1/4 CUP CHOPPED KALAMATA OLIVES, PITTED
1 TEASPOON MINCED FRESH ROSEMARY
1 TEASPOON DRIED OREGANO
4 TABLESPOONS UNSALTED BUTTER
4 SHEETS PHYLLO DOUGH
CELERIAC PUREE (RECIPE FOLLOWS)
ROSEMARY-MUSTARD AIOLI (RECIPE FOLLOWS)
FRESH ROSEMARY FOR GARNISH

1. Cut one rack of lamb into four double lamb chops, being careful to distribute the meat equally between the four portions and getting two bones into each portion. Repeat with the other rack.

2. Place the lamb on a plate and drizzle with 2 Tablespoons olive oil and season with salt and pepper.

3. Heat a medium-sized sauté pan over high heat. Add 2 Tablespoons olive oil and sear the lamb for 1 minute on each side, browning it all the way around. Reserve the lamb and the pan.

4. Combine the feta cheese, sun-dried tomatoes, kalamata olives, remaining

Rack of lamb makes for an elegant presentation in this recipe. An alternative, which I often use at the Inn, is to make this recipe with a loin of lamb. The loin is a boneless cut of very tender meat, and for this recipe, I keep it whole and serve one loin per person. Follow the same procedures for searing the meat, but when it comes to wrapping the loin with phyllo, I use one larger sheet and cover the loin completely. ■

Tablespoon of olive oil, rosemary and oregano together in a small bowl and mix well. Spread the mixture evenly over the top of each double lamb chop.

5. Preheat the oven to 400 degrees.

6. Melt the butter in the same pan used to sear the lamb.

7. Spread out one sheet of the phyllo dough on a cutting board and brush generously with the melted butter. Cover with another sheet of phyllo and brush again with butter. Repeat with the remaining 2 sheets to make a stack of four layers. Cut the layered phyllo sheet in half lengthwise, forming 2 four-layer rectangles. Slice each rectangle into four long strips, lengthwise.

8. Wrap the phyllo around the lamb chops and place them on a baking pan. Brush the phyllo with the remaining butter.

9. Bake the lamb in the preheated oven for 15 minutes.

10. To serve, place a scoop of the celeriac puree in the center of the plate. Interlace the two double lamb chops and place them over the celeriac puree. Spread some of the aioli on the plate and garnish with a fresh sprig of rosemary. Serve with vegetables of your choice.

## Celeriac Puree

> 1½ pounds celeriac (celery root), peeled and cut into ½-inch pieces
> 2 large red-skinned potatoes, peeled and cut into ½-inch pieces
> ¼ cup heavy cream
> 3 Tablespoons unsalted butter
> Kosher salt and white pepper to taste

1. Place the diced celeriac and potatoes in a small saucepan, add 1 teaspoon of salt and cover with cold water by about 1 inch.

2. Bring the pan to a boil, reduce to a simmer, and cook for 15 minutes.

3. Drain off all of the water and return the pan to medium heat, adding the heavy cream and butter. Heat for 5 minutes and mash with a potato masher. Season with salt and white pepper.

### ROSEMARY-MUSTARD AIOLI

1 GARLIC CLOVE
1 LARGE EGG YOLK
2 TEASPOONS FRESH LEMON JUICE
PINCH OF CAYENNE PEPPER
1 TEASPOON MINCED FRESH ROSEMARY
2 TABLESPOONS WHOLE GRAIN DIJON MUSTARD
1/4 CUP EXTRA VIRGIN OLIVE OIL
2 TABLESPOONS CANOLA OIL
KOSHER SALT TO TASTE

1. Mince the garlic and mash it with the side of a large knife (using a little salt) until it becomes a smooth paste. In a small mixing bowl, whisk together the garlic, egg yolk, lemon juice, cayenne, rosemary and Dijon mustard.

2. While whisking the egg mixture vigorously, add the oils in a very slow stream. Whisk constantly, adding the oil slowly until all of the oil is incorporated. Season with salt, cover and reserve.

*Traditional French aioli is nothing more than a garlic-flavored mayonnaise. Two flavors that accompany lamb well are the fragrant evergreen properties of rosemary and the full-bodied flavors of whole grain brown mustard. Change the herbs and seasonings around and you can make an aioli to match almost any dish.* ■

## Wine Notes

*While the recipe calls for merlot, it is cabernet sauvignon that is required for this cut of meat. Cabernet sauvignon from Napa Valley, which is often blended with a little merlot, provides the necessary ripe, black, brambly fruit and rich, velvety tannins that are needed to balance the flavor and texture of the steak.* ■

SERVES 4

4 STEAKS OF YOUR CHOICE (RIB EYE, NEW YORK STRIP, FILET MIGNON, T-BONE, PORTERHOUSE)
2 TABLESPOONS EXTRA VIRGIN OLIVE OIL
2 TEASPOONS MINCED ROSEMARY LEAVES (FRESH OR DRIED)
1 TEASPOON FRESHLY GROUND BLACK PEPPER
1 TEASPOON FINE SEA SALT
4 THICK SLICES OF MERLOT-MUSHROOM BUTTER (RECIPE FOLLOWS)

1. Heat a grill pan (or outside BBQ grill) over high heat. If you like your steaks cooked medium or more, preheat an oven to 350 degrees.

2. Coat the steaks with the olive oil and evenly coat with the rosemary and black pepper.

3. Grill the steaks to your liking and finish the steaks in the oven if you prefer them a little more done.

4. When your steak is done, sprinkle it with the fine sea salt and serve it topped with a slice of the merlot-mushroom butter. Serve with your choice of vegetables and potatoes.

## MERLOT-MUSHROOM BUTTER

½ CUP FINELY CHOPPED YELLOW ONION
8 OUNCES PORTABELLA MUSHROOMS, SMALL DICE
½ CUP MERLOT WINE
½ POUND (16 TABLESPOONS), PLUS 1 TABLESPOON
    UNSALTED BUTTER
2 TABLESPOONS COARSELY CHOPPED ITALIAN PARSLEY
½ TEASPOON KOSHER SALT
¼ TEASPOON BLACK PEPPER

1. Melt the 1 Tablespoon butter in a medium-sized sauté
   pan. Add the onions and cook for 3 minutes. Add the diced mushrooms
   and cook for 5 minutes. Add the merlot and cook until the mixture is dry.

2. Spread the mushroom mixture out on a plate and refrigerate until cool.

3. When cool, place the mushroom mixture in a bowl with the rest
   of the butter and Italian parsley and mix well.
   Season with salt and pepper.

4. Spoon the butter out onto parchment paper, forming a thick
   1½-inch-long log. Roll into a smooth log and set up in the
   refrigerator for 30 minutes.

5. Slice into ¾-inch-thick round slices and bring to room
   temperature just before serving.

# $\mathcal{G}$RILLED SALMON NIÇOISE

SERVES 4

6 PLUM TOMATOES
EXTRA VIRGIN OLIVE OIL
KOSHER SALT AND BLACK PEPPER
1 POUND SMALL POTATOES (YUKON GOLD, PURPLE PERUVIAN,
    SMALL REDS, ETC.)
1 TEASPOON CHOPPED ROSEMARY
1/2 POUND HARICOT VERTS (THIN FRENCH GREEN BEANS) — OR
    USE FIDDLEHEAD FERNS
4 SIX-OUNCE SALMON FILLETS, BONELESS AND SKINLESS
4 EGGS, HARD BOILED AND CUT IN HALF LENGTHWISE
1/2 CUP OLIVES (NIÇOISE OR KALAMATA), PITTED AND HALVED
WHOLE GRAIN MUSTARD DRESSING (RECIPE FOLLOWS)
4 SPRIGS FRESH TARRAGON FOR GARNISH

1. Preheat the oven to 375 degrees. Line a baking sheet with parchment paper and brush the paper with 1 teaspoon of the olive oil.

2. Core and cut the plum tomatoes in half lengthwise and place them cut side up on the baking sheet. Drizzle the tomatoes with 2 Tablespoons of olive oil and sprinkle the tomatoes with kosher salt and freshly ground black pepper. Bake in the preheated oven for 2 hours.

3. Place the small potatoes in a pot and cover with cold water and 1 Tablespoon salt. Bring to a boil and simmer for 10 minutes. Remove immediately from the hot water and cool slightly. Cut the potatoes in half or quarters, depending on their size (you want bite-sized pieces) and place in an ovenproof pan or baking sheet. Drizzle the potatoes with 2 Tablespoons olive oil, salt, pepper and the rosemary. Roast in the 375-degree oven for 20 minutes.

*Spring in Maine would not be complete without the first wild vegetable harvest of the season. Fiddleheads are the top part of immature fronds from the ostrich fern. They are found in early May in the wet lowlands of Maine particularly near shaded rivers and creeks. The flavor of fiddleheads is similar to that of asparagus and they are cooked in a similar manner.* ■

4. Bring 2 quarts of water to a boil with 1 Tablespoon salt. At a boil add the haricot verts and blanch for 1 minute. Remove immediately to an ice bath to cool.

5. Heat a grill pan over high heat. Lightly coat the salmon fillets with olive oil and season with salt and pepper. Grill the salmon for 3 minutes on each side (depending on the thickness of the fillets) or until it is barely cooked through. Don't overcook the salmon or it will dry out.

6. Heat the haricot verts in a small sauté pan with a little olive oil and season with salt and pepper.

7. To serve, place a mound of potatoes in the center of each plate. Top the potatoes with the haricot verts and the grilled salmon fillet. Place 3 roasted tomato halves and 2 egg halves around the salmon and sprinkle with some of the halved olives. Ladle the warm dressing over the salmon and garnish with a sprig of fresh tarragon.

## WHOLE GRAIN MUSTARD DRESSING

2 TABLESPOONS WHOLE GRAIN MUSTARD
2 TABLESPOONS WHITE WINE
2 TABLESPOONS FRESH LEMON JUICE
2 TABLESPOONS CHAMPAGNE VINEGAR
1 TABLESPOON CAPERS, LIGHTLY CHOPPED
1 TEASPOON HERBES DE PROVENCE
1/2 TEASPOON KOSHER SALT
1/8 TEASPOON FRESHLY GROUND BLACK PEPPER
1/4 CUP EXTRA VIRGIN OLIVE OIL
1 TEASPOON EACH HERB (CHIVES, TARRAGON, ITALIAN PARSLEY), COARSELY CHOPPED

1. Place all of the ingredients (except the fresh herbs) in a small saucepan and heat up to a simmer, just before serving.

2. Stir in the fresh herbs and serve.

*Wine Notes*

*White wine with fish should be viewed as a guideline and not a rule. In this case, the bright cherry and strawberry flavors of Californian pinot noirs are the perfect match for the smokiness and weight of the grilled salmon. While many Californian pinot noirs can be on the heavy side, wineries such as David Bruce and Acacia produce wonderfully elegant versions of the grape.* ■

# FLOUNDER "OSCAR" WITH MAINE LOBSTER

SERVES 4

TWO 1¼ POUND LIVE MAINE LOBSTERS
1 POUND ASPARAGUS
4 FIVE-OUNCE PORTIONS OF FLOUNDER
2 EGGS
1 TABLESPOON GRATED PARMESAN CHEESE
2 TEASPOONS CHOPPED FLAT LEAF PARSLEY
KOSHER SALT AND GROUND WHITE PEPPER
ALL-PURPOSE FLOUR
CANOLA OIL FOR FRYING
1 TABLESPOON UNSALTED BUTTER
HOLLANDAISE SAUCE (RECIPE FOLLOWS)

1. Remove the tough white lower sections from the asparagus spears. Peel the lower two to three inches of tough outer skin from the bottom of the asparagus.

2. Fill a large 9-quart stockpot with two inches of water; cover and bring to a boil. Add live lobsters, cover and cook for 10 minutes. Remove from the water and let cool. Bring the water back to a boil and add the asparagus, cooking for about 1 minute, and immediately place in a bowl of ice water to cool.

3. When cool, crack lobsters and remove the meat from the claws, knuckles and tails (discarding the vein). Reserve the tail fin for garnish and discard the remaining shells. Slice the lobster tails in half lengthwise and place all of the lobster meat and the tail fins on a buttered ovenproof pan or plate with sides just large enough to hold the meat in a single layer. Cover with foil and reserve in a warm place.

*Any light, firm-fleshed fish will work in this recipe if flounder is not available. Small flatfish, such as sole and plaice, are particularly ideal but I have also used small grouper and haddock successfully at the Inn. Traditionally, "Oscar" dishes are made with crabmeat, which can also be used in place of the lobster here if desired.* ■

Wine notes

*While the flounder and lobster require a wine with some elegance, the hollandaise needs a little more fruit and acidity. Bouchard's meursault les clous provides the more generous fruit with a little less oak and butter characteristics than similar wines. The crisp acidity and slight mineral quality will add to the flavors of the fish and sauce.* ∎

4. Combine the eggs, Parmesan cheese and 1 teaspoon of the parsley in a small bowl and stir vigorously with a fork to combine well. Place the flounder on a plate and sprinkle with salt and pepper; gently coat with flour.

5. Heat a large sauté pan over medium-high heat. Cover the bottom with a thin layer of canola oil and heat. Dip the floured flounder into the beaten egg and coat well. Gently lay the fish in the hot oil and allow the first side to cook to a golden brown before turning, about 2 minutes. Flip the fish over with a spatula and continue cooking on the other side for 2 minutes. In a separate sauté pan, melt 1 Tablespoon butter and heat the asparagus spears, season with salt and pepper.

6. Arrange the cooked fish on a serving plate or platter and top with the warm lobster meat. Lay the asparagus spears on top and spoon over the hollandaise. Finish by sprinkling with the reserved chopped parsley.

## HOLLANDAISE SAUCE

1/2 CUP UNSALTED BUTTER
2 EGG YOLKS
1 TABLESPOON DRY WHITE WINE
1 teaspoon FRESH LEMON JUICE
KOSHER SALT AND GROUND WHITE PEPPER TO TASTE

1. Place the butter in a small saucepan and melt over low heat. Set another medium-sized saucepan on the stove over high heat with an inch of water in it, bring to a boil and reduce heat to low.

2. In a medium-sized mixing bowl combine the egg yolks and the white wine. Whisk vigorously for about 2 minutes.

3. Place the bowl over the pan of hot water (it should rest on the top of the

saucepan and the bottom of the bowl should not make direct contact with the water) and whisk continuously for about 2 minutes. This is a tricky step. The idea is to heat the egg yolk mixture without turning it into scrambled eggs. If the sauce appears to be thickening too quickly, then remove it from the heat for a few seconds, and whisk it off the heat. When the sauce is warm to the touch and thick, it is ready for the addition of the melted butter.

4. Add the melted butter 1 Tablespoon at a time and whisk in very well before each addition. Finish the sauce with the lemon juice and season with a pinch of white pepper and salt to taste.

# HERB-BREADED SOLE PROVENÇAL

SERVES 4

2 TABLESPOONS, PLUS 1 TEASPOON EXTRA VIRGIN OLIVE OIL
8 PLUM TOMATOES
2 RED BELL PEPPERS
KOSHER SALT, FRESHLY GROUND BLACK PEPPER AND GROUND
    WHITE PEPPER
4 FOUR-OUNCE PORTIONS OF SOLE FILLETS
ALL-PURPOSE FLOUR
2 EGGS
1/2 CUP PANKO BREAD CRUMBS
1/4 CUP CHOPPED FLAT LEAF PARSLEY
1/4 CUP CHOPPED CHIVES
2 TEASPOONS HERBES DE PROVENCE
OLIVE OIL FOR FRYING
1/4 CUP EXTRA VIRGIN OLIVE OIL
1/2 CUP FINELY SLICED RED ONIONS
2 CLOVES GARLIC, MINCED
4 PLUM TOMATOES, CORED, SEEDED AND DICED
1/4 CUP COARSELY CHOPPED PITTED OLIVES
    (COUNTRY MIX, KALAMATA OR NIÇOISE)
1 TEASPOON HERBES DE PROVENCE
1 TABLESPOON CHOPPED FLAT LEAF PARSLEY
1 TABLESPOON CHOPPED CHIVES
1/2 LEMON, JUICED

*Sole is a pretty ambiguous term here in North America. In Europe, the term "sole" refers to a single fish known as the common sole or Dover sole. Here in the states, you will find the term used for any variety of flatfish from flounder to the myriad of "American soles," which really come from a different family but are closely related. There are subtle differences in the tastes and textures of the flesh in these fish, but any type will work well.* ■

1. Preheat the oven to 375 degrees. Line a baking sheet with parchment paper and brush the paper with 1 teaspoon of the olive oil.

## Wine Notes

*Sole, while delicate on its own, will take on the flavors that surround it. This doesn't change the fish, but only adds to its flavor. The wines of Sancerre have the same ability. The delicate sauvignon blanc grape picks up cool, crisp acidity and slight minerality of the region's soil, which adds both depth and elegance to the wine. In the end, it is the freshness of both the grape and the fish that stand out and complement each other.* ■

2. Core the plum tomatoes and cut each in half lengthwise. Place them cut side up on the baking sheet and drizzle them with 2 Tablespoons of olive oil. Sprinkle the tomatoes with kosher salt, freshly ground black pepper and herbes de Provence. Bake in the preheated oven for 2 hours.

3. Burn the skin of the bell pepper over an open flame and place in a plastic bag to steam for 3 minutes. Peel away the charred skin. Cut in half and remove the seeds and stem. Cut into 1-inch pieces.

4. Place the sole on a plate and sprinkle with salt and white pepper; gently coat with flour. Crack the eggs in a small bowl and whisk with a fork. In another bowl, combine the Panko bread crumbs with the herbs. Dip the floured fish into the beaten egg and then into the herb crumb mixture, turning the fish and pressing the crumb mixture into the fish.

5. Preheat the oven to 250 degrees.

6. Heat a large sauté pan over medium-high heat. Cover the bottom with a thin layer of olive oil and heat. Gently lay the breaded fish in the oil and brown, cooking on the first side for about 1 minute or until the crumbs start to turn light brown. Flip over and continue on the other side. Remove the fish to a cookie sheet and keep warm in the oven.

7. Remove the crumbs from the sauté pan with paper towels and return it to medium-high heat. Add the ¼ cup of olive oil to the pan and stir in the sliced onions and garlic; stir for 30 seconds. Add the diced tomatoes, roasted peppers and olives and cook for 2 minutes. Stir in the herbs, lemon juice and season with salt and black pepper.

8. To serve, arrange the sole on a serving plate or platter and top with the sauce. Place the oven-roasted tomatoes around the platter or plate.

# ALMOND-CRUSTED HADDOCK WITH A LEMON-CHIVE BUTTER SAUCE

SERVES 4

4 FIVE-OUNCE PORTIONS FRESH HADDOCK FILLETS
KOSHER SALT AND GROUND WHITE PEPPER
ALL-PURPOSE FLOUR
1 EGG
1/4 CUP PANKO BREAD CRUMBS
1/4 CUP SLICED ALMONDS
CANOLA OIL FOR FRYING
1 TEASPOON CANOLA OIL
1 SHALLOT, MINCED
1/4 CUP DRY WHITE WINE
1/2 CUP HEAVY CREAM
1/4 CUP UNSALTED BUTTER, CUT INTO SMALL PIECES AND SOFT
2 TEASPOONS LEMON JUICE
1 TEASPOON GRATED LEMON ZEST
2 TABLESPOONS CHOPPED CHIVES

1. Place the haddock on a plate and sprinkle with salt and white pepper; gently coat with flour. Crack the egg in a small bowl and whisk with a fork. In another bowl, combine the Panko bread crumbs with the sliced almonds. Dip the floured fish into the beaten egg and then into the almond crumb mixture, turning the fish and pressing the crumb mixture into the fish.

2. Preheat the oven to 350 degrees.

3. Heat a large sauté pan over medium-high heat. Cover the bottom with a thin layer of canola oil and heat. Gently lay the breaded fish in the oil and brown,

cooking on the first side for about 1 minute or until the almonds and crumbs start to turn light brown. Flip over and continue on the other side. Remove the fish to a cookie sheet and finish cooking in the oven for about 5 minutes.

4. Remove the crumbs from the sauté pan with paper towels and return it to medium-high heat. Add the canola oil and minced shallot and stir for 30 seconds. Deglaze with the white wine and reduce until it is almost dry. Add the cream and reduce by half, until the sauce thickens. Remove the pan from the heat and whisk in the soft butter. Add the lemon zest and lemon juice, season with a pinch of white pepper and salt to taste and finish with the chopped chives.

5. To serve, arrange the haddock on a serving plate or platter and top with the sauce.

# Sautéed Veal Medallions with an Almond-Fig Cream

SERVES 4

5 OUNCES DRIED FIGS (OR 4 FRESH FIGS)
1/4 CUP PORT WINE
EIGHT 4-OUNCE VEAL (TOP ROUND) MEDALLIONS
KOSHER SALT AND GROUND WHITE PEPPER
1/4 CUP ALL-PURPOSE FLOUR
CANOLA OIL FOR FRYING
1 SHALLOT, MINCED
1/4 CUP WHOLE ALMONDS
1 CUP HEAVY CREAM
6 SPRIGS FRESH THYME
2 TABLESPOONS UNSALTED BUTTER
1 TEASPOON WHOLE FRESH THYME LEAVES FOR GARNISH

A rather unusual combination for veal, perhaps, but this is one of my personal favorites. The figs and almonds lend so much texture to this dish and really complement the mild flavors in the veal. If you are one of those people who steers clear of veal, pork tenderloin is a terrific substitute and works equally as well, as do chicken breasts. ∎

*In the southern Rhône region,*

*the small town of Gigondas*

*produces wines from a blend of*

*grenache and syrah, more*

*robust than Cotes du Rhône yet*

*more elegant than Chateauneuf*

*du Pape. This wine, with its*

*vibrant red berry fruit and*

*unique white pepper spice, will*

*bring out the best qualities of*

*both the meat and the sauce.*

*Look for Guigal or*

*St. Cosme.* ■

1. Remove the hard stem from the tip of the dried (or fresh) figs. Cut the figs in half and each half into thirds. Place the cut figs into a small bowl and cover with the port wine. Reserve.

2. If the veal medallions are thicker than a ½ inch, pound them gently between two sheets of plastic wrap. Season the veal with salt and pepper and dredge with flour.

3. Heat a large sauté pan over medium-high heat. Cover the bottom with a thin layer of canola oil and heat. Gently lay the floured veal medallions in the pan and sear on each side for 2 minutes. Remove to a plate and cover with foil to keep warm.

4. Place the minced shallot in the pan and stir around for 1 minute. Add the figs and the port wine to the pan along with the almonds. Stir for 1 minute.

5. Add the heavy cream and 2 whole sprigs of thyme. Reduce the cream to the consistency of a thick sauce and remove the thyme sprigs. Stir in the butter and season with kosher salt and white pepper to taste.

6. To serve, place the veal medallions on the serving plate and cover with the sauce. Sprinkle with fresh thyme leaves, garnish with a sprig of fresh thyme and serve with vegetables and starch of your choice.

# Halibut Tapenade

### SERVES 4

4 FIVE-OUNCE PORTIONS OF FRESH HALIBUT FILLET
KOSHER SALT AND GROUND WHITE PEPPER
ALL-PURPOSE FLOUR
OLIVE OIL FOR FRYING
TAPENADE (RECIPE FOLLOWS)
1 TABLESPOON EXTRA VIRGIN OLIVE OIL

## Wine Notes

*Piedmont, Italy's famed red wine appellation produces a small amount of arneis. This white grape is reminiscent of sauvignon blanc, but offers a more distinct floral component and unique stone fruit qualities that can stand up to the intense flavor of olives. Ceretto Blange is one of the best examples of this rare wine.* ■

1 SHALLOT, MINCED
1/4 CUP DRY WHITE WINE
1/4 CUP UNSALTED BUTTER, CUT INTO SMALL PIECES
1/2 LEMON, JUICED
1 TABLESPOON CHOPPED FLAT LEAF PARSLEY

1. Place the halibut on a plate and sprinkle with salt and white pepper; gently coat with flour.

2. Preheat the oven to 350 degrees.

3. Heat a large sauté pan over medium-high heat. Cover the bottom with a thin layer of olive oil and heat. Gently lay the floured fish in the oil and brown, cooking on the first side for about 2 minutes or until a golden brown crust forms. Flip over and continue on the other side. Remove the fish to a cookie sheet and spread a thick, even layer of tapenade on each fillet. Finish cooking the halibut in the oven for about 5 minutes.

4. Return the sauté pan to medium-high heat. Add 1 Tablespoon olive oil and the minced shallot and stir for 30 seconds. Deglaze with the white wine and reduce until it is almost dry. Add the butter and lemon juice and heat until melted. Season with a pinch of white pepper and salt to taste and finish with the chopped parsley.

5. To serve, arrange the halibut on a serving plate or platter and top with the sauce.

## TAPENADE

1 TEASPOON MINCED GARLIC
2 ANCHOVY FILLETS
2 CUPS PITTED OLIVES (COUNTRY MIX OR KALAMATA)
1/2 LEMON, JUICED

1/4 TEASPOON GROUND BLACK PEPPER
1/4 CUP EXTRA VIRGIN OLIVE OIL

1. Combine all of the ingredients but the olive oil in the food processor and blend until well pureed.

2. With the food processor still running, drizzle in the olive oil until it is well combined.

# BRAISED LAMB SHANKS WITH ROSEMARY POLENTA

SERVES 2

1 TABLESPOON EXTRA VIRGIN OLIVE OIL
2 LAMB SHANKS (NEW ZEALAND, ABOUT 3/4 POUND EACH —
   AMERICAN, 1 1/4 TO 1 1/2 POUNDS EACH)
KOSHER SALT AND FRESHLY GROUND BLACK PEPPER
ALL-PURPOSE FLOUR
2 TABLESPOONS UNSALTED BUTTER
1 CUP FINELY DICED CARROTS
1 CUP FINELY DICED YELLOW ONIONS
1 CUP FINELY DICED CELERY
1 LARGE GARLIC CLOVE, MINCED
3 TABLESPOONS TOMATO PASTE
1/4 CUP ALL-PURPOSE FLOUR
1 CUP DRY RED WINE
1/4 CUP PORT WINE, RUBY
2 1/2 CUPS BEEF/VEAL STOCK OR BROTH
1/2 CUP DRIED PORCINI MUSHROOMS
1 SMALL BAY LEAF
ROSEMARY POLENTA (RECIPE FOLLOWS)
2 WHOLE SPRIGS OF FRESH ROSEMARY FOR GARNISH

Osso buco is a dish from the Piedmont region in Italy and literally translates to "bone hole," referring to the marrow track that is exposed when a large veal shank is cut into slices. Lamb shanks are smaller than veal shanks and can be used whole in this dish, if desired. Sliced veal shanks can also be used in this recipe following the same procedures as for the lamb, yielding a slow-braised dish similar to the traditional osso buco. ■

Wine Notes

*While merlot is the most common match for lamb, this particular cut and recipe is better suited to the shiraz grape. South African shiraz offers much of the same fruit qualities as its Australian counterparts but adds certain earth and herb components not found in other regions. Roodeberg and Stellenzicht wineries both offer excellent examples of this South African earthiness.* ■

1. Smaller shanks (New Zealand) can be used whole, while the bigger ones are best cut in half. The lower skinnier part should be tied with kitchen string and the bone frenched.

2. Heat a large ovenproof skillet over medium-high heat. Season the lamb shanks with salt and pepper and dredge with flour. Pour the olive oil into the heated pan and add the floured shanks. Brown the shanks for about 4 minutes, turn and brown the other side. Both sides should be golden brown. Remove the shanks from the pan and return the pan to the stove.

3. Preheat the oven to 350 degrees.

4. Add the butter to the pan and when it melts, add the carrots, onion, celery and garlic. Stir occasionally as the vegetables brown, for about 10 minutes. Add the tomato paste and stir into the vegetables. Cook for about 2 minutes and add the flour. Stir the flour in and cook, stirring for another minute.

5. Deglaze the pan with red wine and stir, working the browned bits off from the bottom of the pan. Add the port, stock, dried mushrooms, bay leaf and the browned lamb shanks and bring the mixture to a boil. Cover the skillet and place in the preheated oven to braise for 1 hour. Remove the pan from the oven, uncover and turn the lamb shanks over. Cover and return to the oven to braise for 1 more hour, or until the meat is very tender. Discard the bay leaf and season the sauce with salt and pepper.

6. Place a spoonful of the rosemary polenta on 2 plates and place a lamb shank over each mound of polenta. Spoon some sauce over the lamb and garnish with the whole sprigs of rosemary. Serve with vegetables of your choice.

## ROSEMARY POLENTA

2 CUPS WATER
1/2 CUP YELLOW CORNMEAL
1/2 TEASPOON KOSHER SALT
1/4 CUP GRATED PARMESAN CHEESE
1 TEASPOON FINELY MINCED FRESH ROSEMARY LEAVES

1. Combine ½ cup of water with the cornmeal and salt.

2. Boil the remaining 1½ cups of water over high heat. At a boil, whisk the softened cornmeal into the water, stirring constantly until thickened. Stir in the Parmesan cheese. Cover and reduce the heat to low, continuing to cook for 5 minutes.

3. Stir in the rosemary just before serving.

# Seared Sea Scallops with Spring Pea Cream and Smoked Salmon

SERVES 4

2 TABLESPOONS, PLUS 1 TEASPOON CANOLA OIL
1 SHALLOT, MINCED
1/4 CUP DRY WHITE WINE
1/2 CUP HEAVY CREAM
1/4 CUP, PLUS 1 TABLESPOON UNSALTED BUTTER,
    CUT INTO SMALL PIECES AND SOFT
1 TEASPOON LEMON JUICE
1 CUP SHELLED FRESH PEAS (OR FROZEN)
KOSHER SALT AND GROUND WHITE PEPPER
2 POUNDS LARGE SEA SCALLOPS
2 CUPS MASHED POTATOES
1 TABLESPOON CHOPPED CHIVES FOR GARNISH
4 OUNCES SMOKED SALMON

1. Heat a small saucepan over medium-high heat. Add 1 teaspoon canola oil and the minced shallot and stir for 30 seconds. Deglaze with the white wine and reduce until it is almost dry. Add the cream and reduce by half, until the sauce thickens. Remove the pan from the heat and whisk in the 1/4 cup of soft butter. Add the lemon juice and season with a pinch of white pepper and salt to taste. Cover and reserve in a warm place.

2. If you are using fresh peas, place them in a small saucepan with the remaining Tablespoon of butter and 1/4 cup water. Bring to a boil and simmer over medium heat for about 3 minutes. For frozen peas, simply heat them in a pan with the butter. Season with salt and white pepper.

*Diver scallops in Maine are some of the best you will find anywhere in the world. The term "diver scallops" refers to a scallop that was harvested by an actual person diving to the bottom of the ocean and hand harvesting usually only the larger specimens. This yields a much cleaner and more uniform product than the large and destructive draggers can conjure up. Diver scallops are also sold "dry," which means they have not been soaked in water or a preservative to extend their shelf life.* ■

Champagne is often considered

a celebratory wine, but it is

also an excellent match with a

variety of foods. Brut

Champagne will have the

vibrant fruit to pair with the

smoked salmon while also

showing enough acidity to

match the sweetness of the

scallops. Veuve Clicquot,

Bollinger and Henriot are

readily available and quite

delicious. ■

3. Place half of the warm peas in a blender with the sauce and blend until smooth. Cover and reserve in a warm place. Cover the remaining peas and reserve in a warm place as well.

4. Remove and discard the side muscle from the scallops. Season the sea scallops with salt and white pepper. Heat a large sauté pan over high heat. Add the remaining 2 Tablespoons canola oil and heat. Gently lay the scallops in the hot oil and sear on each side for about 2 minutes, browning them well. If the scallops are real large, it may be necessary to reduce the heat at this point and cover the pan with foil to cook them through.

5. To serve, place a mound of mashed potatoes in the center of the serving plate. Arrange the scallops around the potatoes and drizzle with the pea cream. Sprinkle with the remaining peas and the chopped chives. Drape a few slices of smoked salmon over the scallops and serve with vegetables of your choice.

# Pistachio-Crusted Pork Medallions with Roasted Apples

### SERVES 4

2 POUNDS PORK TENDERLOIN
KOSHER SALT AND FRESHLY GROUND BLACK PEPPER
¼ CUP ALL-PURPOSE FLOUR
2 LARGE EGGS
¼ CUP COARSELY GROUND PISTACHIOS
¼ CUP PANKO BREAD CRUMBS
3 GRANNY SMITH APPLES
3 TABLESPOONS UNSALTED BUTTER
1 CUP APPLE JUICE
½ CUP BORDELAISE SAUCE (RECIPE, PAGE 37)

CANOLA OIL

2 TEASPOONS CHOPPED ITALIAN PARSLEY FOR GARNISH

## Wine Notes

*This dish offers an interesting*

*blend of flavors and, therefore,*

*needs a rather versatile wine.*

*The tempranillo grape when*

*grown in the warm climate of*

*La Mancha, Spain, shows a*

*red currant fruit and*

*underlying nuttiness along with*

*supple tannins that will not*

*overpower the softer flavors of*

*the pork.* ■

1. Trim fat and silver skin from the pork tenderloin. Cut into eight equal pieces. Working with a few pieces at a time, find a solid counter and place the pork pieces, cut side down, on a sheet of plastic wrap. Cover the top with another sheet of plastic wrap and pound out the pork medallions until they are uniformly $\frac{1}{2}$ inch thick. Continue with all of the pork.

2. Season the pork with salt and pepper and dredge with flour. Crack the eggs into a small bowl and whisk. In another small bowl, combine the pistachios and Panko bread crumbs. Dip a pork medallion into the egg mixture and coat both sides. Let excess egg drip back into the bowl. Dip it into the pistachio/bread crumb mixture next and pat the crumbs onto both sides to coat it well. Continue with the remaining pork. Cover with plastic and refrigerate until ready to cook.

3. Peel and core one of the apples and cut into small dice. Melt 1 Tablespoon of the butter in a small saucepan over medium-high heat. Add the diced apple and cook for 5 minutes, stirring occasionally. Add the apple juice and bordelaise sauce and bring the mixture to a boil. Lower the heat to a simmer and reduce until you achieve a nice thick sauce consistency. Press the sauce through a fine strainer and keep covered and warm until serving.

4. Preheat the oven to 400 degrees. Core the remaining two apples and slice each into $\frac{1}{2}$-inch-thick slices. Melt the remaining 2 Tablespoons of butter and toss with the apple slices. Season with salt and pepper and spread the apple slices out on a parchment-lined baking sheet. Roast in the preheated oven for 20 minutes.

5. Heat a large sauté pan over medium-high heat. Cover the bottom with a thin

layer of canola oil and heat. Gently lay the breaded pork medallions in the oil and brown, cooking on the first side for about 1 minute or until the crust starts to turn light brown. Flip over and continue on the other side. Remove the pork to a cookie sheet and finish cooking in the oven for about 10 minutes.

6. To serve, arrange the pork medallions on a serving plate and top with the sauce and the roasted apples. Sprinkle with parsley and serve with wild rice and vegetable of your choice.

IT'S 5 IN THE MORNING, Bert Witham left the dock at 4:30, a posse of seagulls practically rides his wake, and his VHF radio is crackling with early morning chatter:

> Tommy lost two lines yesterday.
>
> I heard about that.
>
> Looks like we're in for a smooth one today.

Eventually, the caller sneaks in what he's really after. "How many pounds did you bring home yesterday?" That's when the fish tales start flying, and you know you're off to another day of hauling in your lines. One thing's for sure. No lobsterman ever tells another lobsterman the exact nature of his catch. It's simply the way it is.

———

Bert Witham, a Maine lobsterman for the last 55 years, is up at 3:30 and usually in bed by 9. Like his father, and the men in his family for the last five generations, he started catching lobster at a young age. He began with ten traps and tended to them alone, in his skiff with a Martin outboard.

By tenth grade, when Bert was in prep school, his father spotted a 32-foot lobster boat while he was in Nova Scotia. He called Bert, said he thought Bert should have it, Bert agreed, and when the boat arrived, Bert paid for it with the savings he'd accrued to that point.

One summer Sunday, when he was 15, he headed out in his new lobster boat, his "maiden voyage" as Bert likes to call it, from Rockland on his way to Big Green Island, but partway there, he became engrossed in the latest *Superman* comic and when he next looked up was enveloped in a "dungeon-thick fog." It didn't take long for him to realize the predicament he was in. Soon after, a lobster boat came into view and an older fisherman pulled alongside. Bert had seen him occasionally at the docks of his father's sardine factories purchasing bait to re-supply his traps. The fisherman pointed in the direction Bert was to head and said about how many feet he needed to travel before his lobster boat would enter the pathway his uncles would be taking to the island. Bert did

as he was told and, sure enough, his uncles found him and steered him the rest of the way. When Bert's father learned what had happened, he repaid that lobsterman for saving his son's life with free bait the rest of his fishing days.

Bert continued going to school and continued to lobster in his free time and during the summers. Since then, Bert's expanded the number of traps he lays and he's traded up a couple of times, selling his previous boat to his eldest son (both of his sons are in the business of catching lobster), and buying what he calls, with a twinkle in his eyes, his "last boat." And *Lobstar*, all 42 feet of her, is a beauty. He had talked it over with his wife Donni, and told her that he wanted to make this boat everything he'd always wanted in a lobster boat and that's exactly what he did. Among many things, it's light yet stable, which is perfect for one of Bert's passions — Maine lobster boat racing.

Today, with the help of a sternman and occasionally a helper, Bert tends 800 traps, the legal limit, that have been strategically placed off Big Green Island, Maine, which is nine to fourteen miles offshore, depending whether you're lobstering off the near or far side of the island. You can catch Maine lobster year-round, a long season with peaks and valleys and the eternal quest for hauling in the most, but Bert fishes from April through November, and is usually out of the water by December 10th.

That wasn't always the case. The worst day he ever had fishing was with his father when he was 19 or 20 years old. It was 17 below when they started out, and they had hauled traps most of that day. They wore woolen mittens, purposely oversized by the fishermen's wives who knit them, that had been shrunk tight by dipping them first in hot water before letting them cool. Bert remembers grabbing the exhaust pipe off and on in an attempt to keep his hands warm and still recalls the stench of his mittens from all the bait splatter caked on that pipe. He also remembers helping to cut off his father's wedding ring that night because his fingers had become so swollen from the cold.

———

Out fishing one day, Bert spotted a pot buoy going in the opposite direction of what it should be doing, and watched as it continued to move. Puzzled, he caught up with the buoy, and became even more perplexed when his hydraulics weren't strong enough to pull up the traps. He called for help and another 42-foot fiberglass boat in the area

came to assist. With the hydraulics from both boats engaged, they were able to haul up the line and, to their surprise, a 40-foot minke, pale gray with a whitish underside, tangled up in it. Bert thought the whale was dying because it barely fought the hydraulics each time they hauled it to the surface to cut more of the line away. Over half an hour later, they were able to set the whale free, and watch as it swam away.

"You never know what you're going to get when you pull up a line," says Bert. He's found a six-pack of beer in one of his lobster crates, a mitten on the claw of one of the lobsters and he heard recently about an inflatable doll that had been tied on to one of his friend's pot buoys. As that man approached, it appeared that a naked woman was waving to him from atop the bobbing buoy. That is some of the fun that they have on the sea, but a solid fisherman's code underlies it all. Encroachment of someone's lobster area is heavily frowned upon. The first time you do it, you find your buoys tied up, which is called "hitching your tail." The second time, "you're apt not to find them there," says Bert. If you're caught molesting another lobsterman's gear, you go straight to court and usually lose your fishing license. Overall, in any given area, the lobster community is a tight-knit one.

———

As *Lobstar* nears the first marker, Bert, his sternman and the helper, already dressed in orange rubber overalls and rubber boots, stow breakfast drinks, don their work gloves,

stuff mesh bags with sharply pungent bait, and with anticipation of the forthcoming catch, ready themselves for the dance of haul, empty, re-bait and toss. Bert, unfazed about accidentally cutting lines because he had a cage built around the propeller to prevent just that from happening, lets up some on the throttle to position *Lobstar* near his first pot buoy, painted yellow and white because "they're eye-catching — they used to be pink," and engages the on-demand hydraulic wench.

When the first trap, a plastic-coated wire container about four feet long, weighted down with bricks and weighing about 40 to 50 pounds dry and empty, is hoisted onto the ledge of the side of the boat, the sternman pops the lid, eyeballs the catch and throws all the too little or too big lobsters back into the sea. Pleased to see some one and a half pounders, which are roughly seven-year-old lobsters, he tosses the "keepers" and the "maybe's" in the shallow compartments resting on top of the stainless steel bait hold and any crabs into a separate section of the stainless steel lobster hold. He moves the trap toward the helper who re-baits as the sternman empties the second trap before passing it to the helper who re-baits and waits for a nod from Bert. When that happens, the helper lets go and the traps and the line they're on run the ledge at breakneck speed before dropping off the boat's stern where they quickly sink back into the sea.

Twice, Bert has gotten his foot caught in a line on board and been shot to the stern on his way overboard with the traps. Both times, thankfully, his sternman was quick to act, managing to get enough slack in the rope to prevent Bert from being immediately plunged to the depths.

As Bert maneuvers his vessel into position to haul out the next line and its two traps, the helper bags more bait while the sternman finishes measuring the backs of the "maybe's" with a brass measure before tossing those not within the legal size limit back to sea or "V-notching" the tail flippers of any females with eggs (thousands of green eggs attached to the undersides of the tail) before they're thrown back to sea because they're breeders and illegal to sell. Then he bands the claws of each "keeper," so they don't fight in captivity, before he tosses them in the lobster hold.

The timing of these men is perfection; the movements appear synchronized, seamless, a work of art. They continue this dance for hours, with the exception of a quick lunch break, until the traps have been hauled and the 22 bushels of dead herring are gone, and they've scrubbed down and hosed off the sides of the boat, all compartments of the bait hold, the interior walls, the entire deck. Only then do they remove their work gloves, relax a bit and let *Lobstar*'s power steering and 1,000 hp twin-turbo diesel engine practically fly them back to the wharf.

Bert Witham's wharf is a busy place that includes 12 lobster boats in all that sell their catch to Bert, who acts as the middleman, and, in turn, sells most of his lobsters and crabs to the wholesaler Billy Atwood. When Bert and his sternman and helper glide in to the dock, the wharf manager weighs the day's catch before they crate them, drop them in the sea, and call it a day. Having put in a solid 8-hour day, they can't help but feel a little tired. Bert's delightful wife Donni is the bookkeeper and runs the wharf with a computerized system and some dependable, strong help. Overlooking the wharf and a section of Penobscot Bay in Tenant's Harbor is Bert and Donni's lovely, recently renovated home — the house that Bert summered in as a kid.

It's been a few decades since Bert's "maiden voyage" in his first lobster boat. Given the sophisticated electronics on board his boat *Lobstar*, custom built and personally designed by Bert, chances are quite exceptional that he'll never be lost in the fog again. ■

Desserts

# Amaretto Zabaglione with Fresh Berries and Macaroons

SERVES 2

4 LARGE EGG YOLKS, ROOM TEMPERATURE

4 TABLESPOONS AMARETTO (ALMOND LIQUEUR)

3 TABLESPOONS GRANULATED SUGAR

3 CUPS FRESH BERRIES, SLICE STRAWBERRIES IF USING THEM

8 ALMOND MACAROONS, CUT 6 IN HALF AND
    RESERVE 2 WHOLE FOR GARNISH (RECIPE, PAGE 69)

2 SPRIGS FRESH MINT

10 WHOLE ALMONDS, HALVED FOR GARNISH

1. Place the egg yolks, amaretto and sugar in a heat-proof mixing bowl and rapidly whisk (mechanically or manually) for 3 minutes or until frothy.

2. Take the bowl to the stove, and whisk the mixture by hand over medium heat. The key is to heat the mixture (while whisking) without curdling the eggs. As the bowl gets too hot, remove it from the heat, continuing to whisk, and as it cools, return it to the heat and whisk. Whisk until the zabaglione is thick and warm.

3. To serve, alternate layers of zabaglione, berries and macaroon halves between two tall "hurricane" glasses. Garnish the tops with the whole almond macaroons, mint and halved almonds.

(RECIPE, PAGE 69)

*Wine Notes*

*Australian tawny port offers restrained berry fruit with overtones of hazelnuts, caramel and coconut. This is a perfect match for the flavors of this dish.* ■

# Upside-Down Orange and Pistachio Cake

*Step aside, pineapple. Oranges take center stage in this dessert and a final splash of Grand Marnier takes it to another level. I use a Microplane zester/grater for zesting the oranges in this recipe, a culinary tool that no kitchen should be without. Originally designed for woodworking, the graters have now been adapted for kitchen use and are available with various size teeth from fine to real coarse. The zester/grater model with a plastic handle is an all-purpose grater that works well for most uses.* ■

SERVES 6

1 Tablespoon unsalted butter
3 Tablespoons light brown sugar, firmly packed
2 Tablespoons coarsely chopped shelled pistachios
4 large navel oranges
1 cup orange juice
1/4 cup Grand Marnier liqueur
1 1/4 cups all-purpose flour
1/4 teaspoon kosher salt
1 Tablespoon baking powder
1/2 cup granulated sugar
3 eggs, separated
4 Tablespoons unsalted butter, soft
Powdered sugar in a shaker
Vanilla ice cream

1. Butter a 9-inch springform pan with 1 Tablespoon butter and sprinkle with the brown sugar and pistachios.

2. Using a fine Microplane, remove the zest from the oranges and reserve. Remove the remainder of the skin and pith from the oranges with a knife, leaving only the flesh. Cut 3 of the oranges into 1/2-inch slices and remove all the seeds.

3. Lay the orange slices in the bottom of the springform pan, covering the bottom evenly. Cut the slices as necessary to fill in the gaps.

4. Cut the remaining peeled orange into 1-inch seedless pieces and place it in a small saucepan with any of the juices from the cutting board. Add the reserved orange zest along with the orange juice and Grand Marnier liqueur. Place the saucepan on the stove over medium-high heat and reduce the liquid by half. Remove from the heat and cool.

5. Preheat the oven to 350 degrees.

6. In a medium-sized mixing bowl, mix together the flour, salt and baking powder. Make a well and add the sugar, egg yolks, soft butter and the cooled orange reduction. Mix together until combined.

7. In a mixing bowl, whip the egg whites to stiff peaks. Fold the egg whites gently into the batter and pour over the oranges.

8. Bake for about 40 minutes, or until the top is golden brown. Cool on a wire rack. Remove the sides from the springform pan and invert the cake onto a serving plate. Sprinkle with the powdered sugar.

9. Serve warm with a scoop of vanilla ice cream and a splash of Grand Marnier liqueur.

## MICHAEL'S TIRAMISU

SERVES 4

3 LARGE EGGS, SEPARATED
1/2 CUP GRANULATED SUGAR
16 OUNCES MASCARPONE CHEESE
1/2 CUP CHILLED HEAVY CREAM
1 CUP BREWED ESPRESSO, COOLED TO ROOM TEMPERATURE
1/4 CUP KAHLUA (COFFEE LIQUEUR)
HAZELNUT POUND CAKE (RECIPE FOLLOWS)
1 OUNCE BAR BITTERSWEET CHOCOLATE

### Wine Notes

*The rule of thumb for dessert wines is to match the color of the dessert to the color of the wine. Essencia, a muscat-based wine from California, not only offers the appropriate hue, but also evokes aromas of fresh oranges, native spice and toasted nuts. ∎*

3 TABLESPOONS TOASTED, COARSELY CHOPPED HAZELNUTS
2 TABLESPOONS CHOCOLATE COFFEE BEANS (OPTIONAL)

1. Place the egg yolks and ¼ cup of the sugar together in a mixing bowl. Whisk on medium speed for a few minutes until the mixture becomes thick and pale. Add the mascarpone and whisk in well.

2. In another bowl, beat the heavy cream to stiff peaks and reserve in the refrigerator. In another mixing bowl, beat the egg whites to soft peaks. Continue beating as you add the other ¼ cup of sugar. Beat to stiff peaks. Gently fold the whipped cream into the mascarpone mixture and then fold in the beaten egg whites.

3. Gather 4 clear serving bowls — I use small "trifle"-shaped footed bowls.

4. Slice the hazelnut pound cake into ½-inch-thick slices. Mix together the espresso and Kahlua in a small bowl. Dip four slices of the pound cake in the espresso mixture for a second on each side and place the slices in each of the serving bowls. Spoon a few Tablespoons of the mascarpone mixture over each slice of hazelnut pound cake and repeat the process again with a second and third layer. Cover and refrigerate the tiramisu for 4 hours or overnight.

5. Shave the chocolate bar with a vegetable peeler.

6. Just before serving, sprinkle with the chocolate shavings, hazelnuts and chocolate coffee beans.

## HAZELNUT POUND CAKE

### MAKES 2 SMALL LOAVES

1 CUP, PLUS 1 TABLESPOON GRANULATED SUGAR
1 CUP (16 TABLESPOONS) UNSALTED BUTTER, SOFT
4 LARGE EGGS

*Wine Notes*

*A light Moscato d'Asti from Ceretto or Rivetti will add nicely to the richness of this dessert and the slight effervescence will serve as a refreshing palate cleanser.* ▪

1 TEASPOON VANILLA EXTRACT
1 3/4 CUPS ALL-PURPOSE FLOUR
1/2 CUP, PLUS 1 TABLESPOON CRACKED HAZELNUTS

1. Preheat the oven to 350 degrees.

2. Cream the sugar and butter together in a mixer until smooth.

3. Add the eggs and vanilla and mix in. Add the flour and 1/2 cup of the hazelnuts and mix until incorporated.

4. Butter two small loaf pans (2 1/2 cup size) and lightly coat with flour, tapping out the excess flour. Divide the batter between the two pans and sprinkle the tops with the remaining hazelnuts. Bake until a toothpick comes out clean, about 1 hour.

5. Remove from oven and let cool 5 minutes. Remove the loaves from the pans and transfer them to cooling racks to cool.

# MACADAMIA NUT AND GUAVA TARTLETS

SERVES 2

1 CUP MACADAMIA NUTS (PLUS A SMALL HANDFUL FOR GARNISH)
3 TABLESPOONS UNSALTED BUTTER, DICED SMALL AND CHILLED
1 1/2 TABLESPOONS GRANULATED SUGAR
2/3 CUP ALL-PURPOSE FLOUR
1 LARGE EGG YOLK
1 LARGE EGG
1/4 CUP LIGHT BROWN SUGAR, FIRMLY PACKED
2 TABLESPOONS DARK CORN SYRUP
1 TABLESPOON UNSALTED BUTTER, MELTED

*As rich and gooey as a pecan pie, this tartlet features macadamia nuts and guava jelly. Guava is a tropical fruit native to the Caribbean that has a very unique and distinctive flavor and aroma. I can buy guava jelly at my local supermarket in the gourmet aisle. If you can't find it in your area, try to find other tropical fruit jellies, but any flavor will work.* ■

## Wine Notes

*A late-harvest muscat from either California or France will show wonderful notes of orange and citrus fruit with hints of nuts and caramel, a perfect complement to this dessert.* ▪

1. Toast the macadamia nuts in a preheated 350-degree oven for 10 minutes.

2. Crust: Place ½ cup of the toasted macadamia nuts in the bowl of a food processor and process until fine. Add the butter, sugar and flour and process until the mixture forms a coarse meal. Add the egg yolk and mix just until combined. The crust mixture will be very coarse and crumbly. Divide the mixture in half and press into two 4-inch tartlet pans with removable bottoms.

3. Preheat the oven to 350 degrees.

4. Filling: Combine the egg, brown sugar, corn syrup, melted butter and vanilla and whisk until well mixed.

5. Spread each tartlet shell bottom with 1 Tablespoon of the guava jelly. Divide the remaining macadamia nuts (reserving the handful for garnish) between the two tartlet shells and cover each tartlet with half of the filling.

6. Bake in the preheated oven for 40 minutes, until the tarts begin to puff. Remove from the oven and let cool 10 minutes.

7. Serve warm with a large scoop of vanilla ice cream, a sprinkling of toasted macadamia nuts and a sprig of fresh spearmint.

# TANGERINE CRÈME CARAMEL WITH PLUMPED APRICOTS

SERVES 4

## CARAMEL

> ¹/4 CUP GRANULATED SUGAR
> 1¹/2 TABLESPOONS WATER

1. Combine the sugar and water in a small saucepan and place over high heat. Cook, without stirring, until the sugar turns a golden brown.

2. Immediately pour the caramel into the bottom of four small (175 ml or 6-ounce) glass ramekins, dividing the mixture evenly between them. Work quickly or the caramel will set up and you won't be able to pour it.

## PLUMPED APRICOTS

> 2 FRESH TANGERINES
> ¹/2 CUP GRANULATED SUGAR
> ¹/4 CUP LIGHT CORN SYRUP
> ¹/4 CUP GRAND MARNIER LIQUEUR
> 1 CUP WATER
> 16 DRIED APRICOTS

1. Peel the skin from the tangerines using a vegetable peeler and reserve for the Candied Tangerine Peel (recipe follows).

2. Juice the tangerines and place the juice in a small saucepan, making sure there are no pits. Add the sugar, corn syrup, Grand Marnier and water in a medium

## Wine Notes

*Sauternes is the most famed
of all dessert wines and with
good reason. The flavors are
multilayered, with notes of
citrus, apricot, lemon drop and
honey. The best are sweet but
not cloying and offer intense
acidity. They can also be very
expensive but there are great
values from Chateau Liot and
La Fleur d'Or.* ■

(4 quart) saucepan and bring to a boil over medium-high heat. Add the dried apricots and cover the pan. Poach the apricots for 5 minutes, plumping them. With a slotted spoon, carefully remove the apricots from the pan and spread them out on a plate to cool.

3. Reduce the tangerine juice over medium-high heat until it has reduced to about ¼ cup and reserve for the custard (recipe follows).

## CUSTARD

> 1 CUP HEAVY CREAM
> ½ CUP MILK
> ½ VANILLA BEAN, CUT LENGTHWISE AND SEEDS SCRAPED OUT
> TANGERINE REDUCTION (FROM THE PLUMPED APRICOTS,
>     RECIPE ABOVE)
> ¼ CUP GRANULATED SUGAR
> 2 EGGS
> 1 EGG YOLK

1. Preheat the oven to 350 degrees and bring some water to a boil in a teakettle or saucepan for the water bath.

2. Combine the heavy cream, milk, scraped vanilla bean and tangerine reduction (from Step 3 above) in a medium-sized saucepan and bring to a simmer.

3. In a medium-sized bowl, whisk together the sugar, eggs and egg yolk.

4. When the cream mixture simmers, whisk it slowly into the egg mixture. Strain the mixture through a fine mesh strainer and divide the custard between the four prepared ramekins. Place the filled ramekins in a baking pan with tall sides and fill the pan with the boiling water, reaching halfway up the sides of the ramekins. Place in the center of the preheated oven and bake for 40 minutes or until the custard firms up. Refrigerate for at least 2 hours before serving.

## CANDIED TANGERINE PEEL

TANGERINE PEEL (RESERVED FROM THE PLUMPED APRICOTS
RECIPE, PAGE 193)
1/2 CUP GRANULATED SUGAR

1.  Using a sharp knife, remove as much of the white pith as possible from the tangerine skin. The white pith is very bitter, so removal is imperative.

2.  Slice the skin into very thin strips and place in a small saucepan with 1 cup of cold water. Bring to a boil, drain off the liquid, and continue again with another cup of cold water. Continue this blanching three times.

3.  Drain off the last of the water and place ¼ cup of the sugar in the saucepan with the tangerine peel along with ¼ cup of cold water. Place the pan over medium-high heat and reduce, stirring, until all of the liquid is gone.

4.  Turn the peel out onto a piece of parchment paper and toss with the remaining ¼ cup of granulated sugar. Let dry for about 1 hour and place in a covered container until serving. Store at room temperature.

## TO SERVE

WHIPPED CREAM
4 SPRIGS FRESH SPEARMINT

1.  Loosen the custard from the ramekins by carefully inserting a thin knife along the outside rim and rotating the ramekins to break the seal. Invert the ramekins over the center of the serving plates and the custard should fall right out. Remove the ramekins.

2.  Divide the plumped apricots between the four plates, resting one on top of each custard. Sprinkle the plates with the candied tangerine peel and garnish with a dollop of whipped cream and a sprig of fresh mint.

# CHOCOLATE-ALMOND TORTE WITH ALMOND MACAROONS

MAKES 4 TORTES

1/4 CUP CRUSHED ALMOND MACAROONS (RECIPE, PAGE 69)
2 TABLESPOONS COARSELY CHOPPED TOASTED ALMONDS
1/2 CUP COCOA POWDER, SIFTED
PINCH KOSHER SALT
1/2 CUP (4 OUNCES) SEMI-SWEET CHOCOLATE CHIPS
1/2 CUP (8 TABLESPOONS) UNSALTED BUTTER, SOFT
1/2 CUP GRANULATED SUGAR

1/2 TEASPOON ALMOND EXTRACT
3 LARGE EGGS
4 LARGE SCOOPS VANILLA ICE CREAM
8 ALMOND MACAROONS (RECIPE, PAGE 69)
4 SPRIGS FRESH MINT
20 WHOLE ALMONDS, HALVED FOR GARNISH

1. Preheat the oven to 350 degrees. Butter 4 (1½ cup) soufflé cups and place a small round of buttered parchment in the bottom of each.

2. Combine the almond macaroons, almonds, cocoa powder and salt in the bowl of a food processor and process until it is ground to a fine meal.

3. Place the chocolate and butter in a small "microwave safe" glass bowl and melt in the microwave, stirring it every 20 seconds, until it is completely melted.

4. Add the sugar, almond extract and eggs to the food processor and mix until smooth. Add the melted chocolate and mix until smooth.

5. Divide the cake mixture between the prepared soufflé cups and place on a cookie sheet. Bake in the center of the preheated oven for 30 minutes.

6. Remove from the oven and cool the ramekins on a cooling rack. After 10 minutes, flip each cake out into your hand and remove the parchment paper. The tortes can be prepared up to 3 days in advance and kept refrigerated until needed.

7. Warm the cake slightly before serving. Place the tortes off center on the plates and add a large scoop of vanilla ice cream. Garnish with the almond macaroons, mint and halved almonds.

*H*

*Wine Notes*

*France's version of port is known as banyuls. Produced deep in Southern France, this fortified wine shows incredible concentrated red berry fruit with not-so-subtle overtones of bittersweet chocolate. Clos de Paulilles banyuls is definitely worth the search for this dessert.* ■

## Chocolate Molds

WHEN YOU HAVE A REAL passion for collecting items, you can look back with fond memories to the specific circumstances related to the discovery and procurement of each item in your collection. When I was a young boy, I collected beer cans. My Grandpa Russell helped me build shelving on all four walls of my bedroom to hold the collection and I could lay in my bed at night and marvel at it. I would remember particular things about each can: the bicycling trip to Iowa with my friend Drew in search of cans, my brother Dave returning from a class trip to Germany with my first foreign cans, trips to Andy's Liquor Store in my hometown of Rochester, Minnesota, to rummage through their shelf of cans for collectors. When I moved away from home, I had to sell my beer can collection (it really wouldn't have traveled well); I was on to a new chapter in my life and cooking was now the focus.

An interest was sparked in old kitchenwares when my Grandma Jean gave me a carving set with horn handles and a glass rolling pin that had been in the family for generations. In my early twenties, I came across my first bunny chocolate mold at an antique store and I realized that I had found my niche. Whenever I traveled from that point on, I would search out antique shows and markets, purchasing every chocolate mold I happened upon. After years of collecting, my eye for old and unusual molds became more discerning, and I passed over the more common pieces. Easter and Christmas were the big holidays for chocolate molds, so I would find molds of Easter bunnies, eggs, chicks, Santa Claus and Father Christmas quite often. These holidays do, however, offer up some unusual molds like the bunny riding a motorcycle or Santa riding a donkey. A trip to Belgium back in 1999 led me to a gentleman whose father had purchased all of the tin chocolate molds from several chocolate factories when they switched to the more efficient plastic molds. Looking through a shop with thousands upon thousands of unique chocolate molds was an overwhelming experience. After many hours, Mary Jo was ready to see more of Brussels than just the inside of that one store, while I could have spent the whole day there.

In recent years, chocolate molds have become more and more collectible, and prices for unique pieces have gone through the roof. The internet, e-Bay in particular, has made collecting easier in some ways, but much more competitive. With any collection, the collector must set up boundaries and limitations, whether it's from a financial or storage standpoint, so recently, I have focused my chocolate mold search to those with an affinity to the sea. Most of my molds are displayed on shelves in the kitchen at the Inn, with my collection of seafood molds displayed in my newly renovated kitchen at home. As I put up the new shelf for my molds, I couldn't help but think of my Grandpa Russell and wish he were here to help me display my new collection.

During the holidays, both Easter and Christmas, I gather a few select molds, start chopping chocolate and make a display of the molds and their magical chocolate creations for our guests to see.

## USING ANTIQUE CHOCOLATE MOLDS

The first step required in using chocolate molds is to temper the chocolate.

Chocolate is tempered to make it more stable. The tempering process involves melting and cooling the chocolate in a specific way to make it more glossy and smooth.

Chocolate that is not tempered can develop a gray streaking called "bloom" and is caused by a crystallization of the fat (cocoa butter) that is found in chocolate. The classical method of tempering chocolate is rather involved and uses a marble slab to cool the chocolate. The following method is much quicker and works quite well. The chocolate can be melted gently over a double boiler if you don't care to use a microwave.

## TEMPERING CHOCOLATE

1. Chop the chocolate into small pieces the size of peas.

2. Place ⅔ of the chocolate in a microwave-safe bowl and place in the microwave for 30 seconds at high power. Remove the bowl from the microwave and stir the chocolate. Return the bowl to the microwave for another 30 seconds, stir and continue this process just until the last chunks melt and the chocolate is smooth.

3. Meanwhile, finely chop the remaining chocolate until it is quite fine. Stir the chopped chocolate into the melted chocolate and stir it for 5 minutes to make it smooth and stable. Keep the chocolate in a warm (not hot) place until ready to use.

## MOLDING CHOCOLATE

Make sure your tin molds are clean and free of rust. If you are using a mold for the first time, it is best to rub the inside of the mold with some neutral cooking oil (canola or vegetable oil) and remove it completely with dry paper towels. This will help prevent the chocolate from sticking to the mold. Chocolate molds can be divided into two categories: flat one-sided molds and three-dimensional molds.

The flat molds are pretty straightforward. Pour the tempered chocolate into the molds and refrigerate briefly until set. Remove the molds from the refrigerator and tap the inverted mold on a solid counter to release the chocolates.

Three-dimensional molds are a little more complicated. Most of these molds have two sides that are simply clipped together and create a chocolate figure that can be viewed from all sides. More complicated molds have hinging bottoms and sides and seem more like puzzles than kitchen utensils. I have a bell mold like this that is composed of 5 moving parts with 3 hinges and 3 clasps and produces two beautiful chocolate bells. These three-dimensional molds can make either solid or hollow chocolate figures.

SOLID FIGURES are the simplest to produce. Clip the mold together and make sure it makes a tight seal. I sometimes wrap a mold tightly with plastic wrap to help hold it together. Invert the mold in a container that will hold it upside down with the hollow "filling hole" exposed. I find that plastic containers from yogurt or from deli purchases hold the molds well and I usually balance them with a wad of aluminum foil. Pour the tempered chocolate into the molds and fill to the top. Gently tap the molds a few times to remove any air bubbles in the chocolate. Refrigerate the molds for awhile (30 minutes for small molds and several hours for large ones) to accelerate the hardening of the chocolate. Remove the molds from the refrigerator and unclip the molds. Gently remove the tin sides from the chocolate and trim away any excess chocolate from the seams.

HOLLOW FIGURES are a little more complicated. Follow the procedures for the solid figures up to the refrigeration of the molds. For the hollow figures, refrigerate the molds for about 5 minutes just to set up the chocolate on the sides of the molds, and then remove it from the refrigerator. Pour out any excess chocolate and return the mold to the refrigerator until completely hardened. If you want a bottom on the mold, spread a little chocolate on a flat plate and place the hardened mold (still in the tin) on top to form a bottom. Return to the refrigerator to set up. Remove the molds from the refrigerator and unclip the molds. Gently remove the tin sides from the chocolate and trim away any excess chocolate from the seams. ■

Cooking Classes

# Chef Michael's Favorite Spices

*I* HAVE PUT TOGETHER A SAMPLER of some of my favorite spices and spice blends that I use on a regular basis. Below are some descriptions of the various spices, references to recipes in both my cookbooks, and some new recipes that utilize these various spices. All of these spice mixtures are available for sale at the Inn or they can be shipped to you directly. Call us at the Inn to place an order or browse at the "Hartstone Marketplace" on our website.

**CUMIN SPICE MIX:** My cumin spice mix is a combination of various spices mixed with brown sugar. The recipe for the cumin spice mix is on page 128 (page 61 in my first cookbook) and is, by far, our biggest seller. I use this mixture extensively at the Inn — for example, sprinkling it over thick-sliced, apple wood-smoked bacon during its final few minutes of cooking or baking squash with a coating of unsalted butter and a generous sprinkling of the cumin spice mix. In this cookbook, I use this blend when roasting the pears for the Baby Spinach Salad (recipe, page 127) and in the Baked Brie with Hazelnuts and Frangelico (recipe, page 254), which is out of this world.

**FENNEL SPICE MIX:** As one of the first recipes developed for this cookbook, fennel spice mix also sees a lot of use at the Inn. The recipe for this blend is on page 59 and is used in numerous recipes throughout this cookbook — from the Maine Lobster and Scallop Terrine (recipe, page 215) to the Prosciutto-Wrapped Jumbo Shrimp (recipe, page 256). My Italian Breakfast Sausage (recipe, page 58) is simply ground pork that is mixed with white wine and the fennel spice mix and formed into patties that I sear and serve at breakfast. This sausage mixture is also great in spaghetti sauce over pasta, after it has been cooked and finely ground. It can also be stuffed into portabella mushroom caps, bell peppers or hollowed out tomatoes that are then baked. Fennel spice mix is also excellent on all kinds of seafood.

**HERBES DE PROVENCE:** This is a mixture of flowery lavender and sweet French and Italian herbs, including savory, rosemary, cracked fennel, thyme, basil, tarragon and marjoram. I use this mixture with poultry: Coat a whole chicken with the herbs and roast it. Or coat a chicken breast with Panko bread crumbs seasoned with herbes de Provence, kosher salt and cracked black pepper and pan fry in medium-hot olive oil for 2 minutes on each side and finish in a preheated 350-degree oven for 15 minutes. In my first cookbook, I use herbes de Provence in the recipe for Pan-Seared Duck Breast (page 143) and in this cookbook you will find it in the recipes for Zucchini-Wrapped Jumbo Shrimp (recipe, page 108), Salmon Niçoise (recipe, page 153) and Sole Provençal (recipe, page 159).

**CHEF MICHAEL'S CARIBBEAN DRY SPICE MIX:** My Caribbean spice mix is a mixture of 13 herbs and spices. The recipe for the spice mix is on page 169 in my first cookbook. I use this mixture often at the Inn to give certain dishes a Caribbean flair with a little bit of heat. In my first cookbook, you will find several recipes that use the spice including Seared Maine Diver Scallops (recipe, page 134), Caribbean Tenderloin of Pork (recipe, page 89) and Jerk-Seared Tuna (recipe, page 180). I also add this spice mix to a dry cure mix (this cookbook, recipe, page 274) when I smoke my Caribbean Smoked Salmon and it is equally great on poultry, seafood and pork.

**CAJUN SPICE MIX:** The recipe for my Cajun spice mix can be found on page 252 (page 151 in my first cookbook) and is quite hot. It is great on blackened foods (chicken, firm fish, and pork) and I used it in my first cookbook on Cajun-Seared Tenderloin of Beef (recipe, page 150). This a great dish that highlights the versatility of this spice mix. In this cookbook, you will find it used in the Spicy Beef Toasts with a Smoked Tomato Confit (recipe, page 251), the Pork and Artichoke Pâté with Pistachios (recipe, page 211) and as a rub in the Smoking Foods section.

**ANNATTO SEED:** I was first introduced to annatto (also known as achiote and ruku) while working in the Caribbean. Annatto is used to color various foods and imparts no flavor. Here in the U.S., annatto is used to color butter and cheese, while in the Caribbean, it is used in many dishes from chicken and fish to rice and grains. Annatto is fat-soluble, so to release its bright color it must be heated in fat or oil. Grind the whole triangular seeds in a spice grinder or make an annatto oil with 1 cup canola oil and 1 teaspoon whole seeds by heating them over low heat until the oil turns red. Annatto oil can be used in place of other oils in any recipe where a red coloring is desired. My recipe for Annatto Grilled Shrimp is on page 177 in my first cookbook.

**STAR ANISE:** One of the most beautiful and fragrant spices in the world, these perfect 8–12 pointed stars are the fruit of the native Chinese evergreen and pack a sweet and dense licorice flavor. In my first cookbook, I use star anise to make a Raspberry-Star Anise Sauce (recipe, page 48), which is used over Poached Pears (recipe, page 47). Another great use for star anise is to make a "spiced sugar" by storing 2 stars in 1 cup of granulated sugar with one-half vanilla bean. Sprinkle this spiced sugar over sautéed fruits (apples, pears, bananas) or over freshly baked pastries.

**CHINESE FIVE SPICE POWDER:** A mixture of cinnamon, star anise, anise seed, ginger and cloves, Chinese five spice powder is a unique blend with a very distinctive flavor. When Julia Child came for dinner at the Inn in August 2001, I prepared a semi-boneless quail for her as an appetizer that was marinated with Chinese five spice powder (recipe, page 31). Other recipes in this cookbook using Chinese five spice powder are Crispy Whole Fish (recipe, page 236) and the Peking Duck hors d'oeuvres (recipe, page 261).

**ROSEMARY STEAK RUB:** This is a simple mixture of kosher salt, black pepper, granulated garlic and rosemary that is great rubbed on steaks, roasts, lamb racks or loins, whole roast chickens — *before* you cook them. Drizzle the meat with a little olive oil, rub in a generous amount of rosemary steak rub and grill, roast or sear. The recipe is located on page 283 in the Smoking Foods section.

**APPLE PIE SPICE MIX:** In the fall, I use this spice mix a great deal. For example, to make a spiced crème Anglaise, simply add 1 teaspoon of the spice mix to 1 batch of crème Anglaise (recipe, page 40, in this cookbook) along with 2 Tablespoons Amaretto. Mix well. Spiced crème Anglaise is good with Spice Baked Apples: core apples, stuff with a mixture of brown sugar, apple pie spice mix, walnuts and raisins, then brush the outside of the apples with egg whites and roll in a mixture of sugar and apple pie spice mix — bake for 20 minutes in a preheated 350-degree oven). It is also good with Fruit Fritters (use apples — recipe, page 54, in my first cookbook). In this cookbook, I use this spice mix in the Apple Tarts (recipe, page 56) and in my Cranberry and Apple Crunch French Toast (recipe, page 50).

**CURRY POWDER:** Curry powder comes in many different varieties; some are mild and some are hot. The one I use in most of my recipes is a mild curry powder and is a mixture of turmeric, coriander, cumin, fenugreek, ginger, nutmeg, fennel, cinnamon, white pepper, cardamom, cloves, black pepper and cayenne pepper. The yellow color of curry powder comes from the turmeric. Several recipes in my first cookbook use curry powder — Chicken Satay (recipe, page 235) and Coconut Chicken/Mussel Soup with Curry (recipe, page 228). Curry is an acquired taste, so use less at first, and as you develop a liking for the taste, you can add more.

**CRYSTALLIZED GINGER:** Crystallized ginger comes from peeled, diced and sugar-cured Australian ginger. Crystallized ginger retains its texture and "warmth" when baking, which makes it perfect for my Ginger Snaps (recipe, page 73, in my first cookbook).

# Pâtés & Terrines

THE WORDS PÂTÉ AND TERRINE usually conjure up visions of complicated recipes and techniques, far beyond the grasp of a typical home cook. To a certain extent, this can be true. Special ingredients, equipment and techniques are required for many of the elaborate preparations, so I have devised a few pâté and terrine recipes that are more "user-friendly" and within the grasp of home cooks. With a price fixe menu at the Inn, it is imperative that I prepare foods that will be appealing to all of my guests. I have to refrain from using certain ingredients like liver and other offal, which are not widely popular. Therefore, the three recipes I chose for this section are liver free and can be enjoyed by all. Each of the recipes can be prepared in small ramekins for individual service or they can be made in loaf pans and sliced for a varied presentation. Each recipe also has its own unique sauce to accompany it.

# PORK AND ARTICHOKE PÂTÉ WITH PISTACHIOS

4 WHOLE ARTICHOKE HEARTS
1 TABLESPOON OLIVE OIL
2 TEASPOONS DRY WHITE WINE
KOSHER SALT AND GROUND BLACK PEPPER
1 TEASPOON UNSALTED BUTTER
1/4 CUP CHOPPED YELLOW ONION
1 CLOVE GARLIC, MINCED
8 OUNCES PORK, COARSELY GROUND (FATTY PORK, LIKE PORK BUTT)
1/2 BEATEN EGG
2 TABLESPOONS HEAVY CREAM
1/4 TEASPOON DRIED BASIL
1/4 TEASPOON PÂTÉ SPICE (RECIPE FOLLOWS)
1/4 TEASPOON CAJUN SPICE MIX (RECIPE, PAGE 252)
1/8 TEASPOON GROUND WHITE PEPPER

*Pork butts (also known as Boston butts) come from the shoulder of a pig and are a perfect cut for making charcuterie of all types, from sausages to pâtés. The butt is marbled with lots of fat, which translates into finished products that are moist and tender. These properties also make the pork butt an excellent cut for pot roasts and slow-cooked pulled pork.* ∎

*Pâté is a complex blend of*

*tastes and textures, all neatly*

*compressed into one simple*

*slice. The best will bring forth a*

*different flavor with each bite,*

*so a wine of similar complexity*

*is needed. In this case, the*

*bold, well-integrated style of*

*a Crozes Hermitage will stay*

*in step with the multilayered*

*personality of this pâté.* ∎

¹/2 TEASPOON KOSHER SALT

1 TABLESPOON CHOPPED PISTACHIOS

8 SLICES "THICK SLICE" BACON (GET SPECIALTY SMOKED,
   LIKE APPLE-WOOD SMOKED, ETC.)

4 SLICES WHOLE GRAIN BREAD

RASPBERRY CUMBERLAND SAUCE (RECIPE, PAGE 215)

A FEW BABY GREENS FOR GARNISH

A FEW ORANGE SEGMENTS FOR GARNISH (FROM RASPBERRY
   CUMBERLAND SAUCE RECIPE)

1. Place the artichoke hearts in a small bowl and coat with the olive oil, white wine and a sprinkle of kosher salt and black pepper.

2. Heat a small sauté pan over medium-high heat. Add the butter and then the onions. Cook, stirring frequently, until the onions start to turn brown. Add the garlic and cook for another minute. Remove the onions to a medium-sized mixing bowl and cool.

3. When the onions are cool, add the ground pork, egg, heavy cream, spices, salt and pistachios. Mix well to combine.

4. Preheat the oven to 350 degrees.

5. Line four 4-ounce ramekins with the sliced bacon by cutting 2 pieces of bacon into 4 pieces each, covering the bottom of each ramekin with 2 of these pieces. Take four whole slices of bacon and run them around the inside sides of the ramekins.

6. Fill the mini pâtés by spooning a heaping Tablespoon of the filling into each ramekin. Smooth the mixture into the bottom of the ramekin and insert a drained artichoke heart, base side down, into the center of each ramekin. Spoon the remaining mixture around and over the artichoke, filling the ramekin and packing it in firmly to avoid air pockets.

7. Cut the remaining 2 slices of bacon into 4 pieces each and place 2 halves over the tops of each pâté, enclosing it neatly in bacon.

8. Place the ramekins in a shallow baking dish and fill with hot water, halfway up the sides. Bake in the center of the preheated oven for 45 minutes. Remove and cool for 5 minutes. Invert the ramekins over a bowl (to catch the juices) and release the pâtés from the ramekins.

9. The pâté can be made up to 4 days in advance and kept covered in the refrigerator until serving.

10. To serve, cut the whole grain bread with seasonal (snowflakes, fall leaves, flowers, hearts) cookie cutters and toast on each side. Slice each pâté in half from top to bottom. Place the two pieces just off center on each plate and open up a wedge of space between them. Spoon a heaping Tablespoon of the raspberry cumberland sauce on the exposed plate between the two halves. Garnish the plates with a few baby greens, a fan of orange segments and the toasted whole grain bread shapes.

## PÂTÉ SPICE

> 5 BAY LEAVES
> 1 TABLESPOON GROUND CLOVES
> 1 TABLESPOON GROUND WHITE PEPPER
> 1 TABLESPOON GROUND BLACK PEPPER
> 1 TABLESPOON SWEET PAPRIKA
> 2 TEASPOONS GROUND NUTMEG
> 2 TEASPOONS GROUND GINGER
> 1 TEASPOON DRIED THYME
> 1 TEASPOON GROUND CORIANDER
> 1 TEASPOON DRIED BASIL

*Pâté spice is not a blend you can pick up at the corner grocery. In fact, you would be hard pressed to find it in a specialty gourmet shop. I find that this combination of spices is uniformly pleasant in most of the meat-based pâtés and terrines I make.* ■

1. Finely grind the bay leaves in a spice grinder and add the remaining ingredients. Mix well.

2. Store in a jar with a tightly sealed lid.

## RASPBERRY CUMBERLAND SAUCE

1/4 CUP RASPBERRY JAM
SEGMENTS FROM 1/2 FRESH ORANGE (RESERVE HALF
    FOR GARNISH)
1/2 TEASPOON FINELY GRATED ORANGE ZEST
2 TEASPOONS PORT WINE

1. Cut the orange segments into small pieces and mix all of the ingredients together.

2. Keep covered and chilled until serving.

## MAINE LOBSTER AND SCALLOP TERRINE WITH A ROASTED PEPPER COULIS

TWO 1 1/2 POUND LIVE MAINE LOBSTERS
8 OUNCES SEA SCALLOPS
1 EGG WHITE
2 TABLESPOONS HEAVY CREAM
1 TEASPOON LEMON JUICE
1/4 TEASPOON LEMON ZEST
1/2 TEASPOON FENNEL SPICE MIX (RECIPE, PAGE 59)
1 TEASPOON CHOPPED CHIVES
1 RED BELL PEPPER
2 CUPS FRESH SPINACH LEAVES

*Cumberland sauce is a fruit-based sauce traditionally made with red currants and served to accompany red meats. In this simple version, I have substituted raspberries for the currants; however, any flavored jam or jelly can be used.* ■

*When is a mixture of forcemeat a pâté and when is it a terrine? I find that most people are confused with this terminology, so let's clarify it. Pâté is the general term for minced meat and fat cooked in a mold. The term "terrine" comes into play when the pâté is cooked in an earthenware "terrine" mold and is actually served in the mold. When a terrine is removed from its mold, it officially becomes a pâté. I generally prepare this seafood pâté in an earthenware mold.* ■

1.  Fill a large 9-quart stockpot with two inches of water; cover and bring to a boil. Add the live lobsters, cover and cook for 6 minutes. Remove from the water and let cool. When cool, crack the lobsters and remove the meat from the claws, knuckles and tails (discarding the vein). Cut the tail fin in half with a pair of kitchen shears and reserve for garnish. Discard the remaining shells. Slice the lobster tails in half lengthwise (reserve) and cut the remaining lobster meat into ½-inch pieces.

2.  Place the sea scallops in the bowl of a food processor. Pulse until the mixture is smooth. Add the egg white and pulse to combine. Add the heavy cream, lemon juice, lemon zest, fennel spice mix and chives and pulse until combined. Remove to a bowl and stir in the chopped lobster meat.

3.  Burn the skin of the bell pepper over an open flame and place in a plastic bag to steam for 3 minutes. Peel away the charred skin. Cut the pepper in half and remove the seeds and stem. Cut each half into two 2-inch circles.

4.  Fill a large bowl with 2 cups of ice and 2 cups of cold water. Bring a quart of water to a boil in a large sauté pan. Blanch the spinach by submerging it in the boiling water for 15 seconds, and then remove it immediately to the ice water to cool it for 3 minutes. Remove the spinach from the water and spread out the leaves between layers of kitchen towels to dry.

5.  Butter four 4-ounce ramekins and line the sides of the ramekins with the dried spinach leaves, leaving the bottoms open. Place a lobster tail half (red side down) in the bottom of each ramekin, and cover with a heaping Tablespoon of the scallop mixture. Spread the mixture evenly over the lobster tail and top with the red pepper round. Top with the remaining scallop mixture, filling each ramekin and packing it firmly to avoid air pockets.

6. Place the ramekins in a shallow baking dish and fill with hot water, halfway up the sides. Bake in the center of the preheated oven for 30 minutes. Remove and cool for 5 minutes. Invert the ramekins over a bowl (to catch the juices) and release the terrines from the ramekins. Discard the juices.

7. The terrine can be made a day in advance and kept covered in the refrigerator until serving.

8. To serve, slice each terrine in half from top to bottom. Place the two pieces just off center on each plate and open up a wedge of space between them. Spoon the roasted pepper coulis on the plate between the two terrine halves and garnish the plates with a few baby greens and the reserved tail fin half.

## Wine Notes

*The bold tropical fruit of Californian chardonnay is sometimes masked by more than adequate oak treatment. In its pure form, it is the perfect accompaniment to this lightly spiced seafood treat. Look for vibrant un-oaked chardonnay from either the vineyards of Clos La Chance or Pellegrini.* ◼

## ROASTED PEPPER COULIS

1/2 SMALL RED ONION
2 CLOVES GARLIC
1 SHALLOT
1/4 CUP EXTRA VIRGIN OLIVE OIL
KOSHER SALT AND GROUND BLACK PEPPER
1 RED BELL PEPPER
1/4 TEASPOON FENNEL SPICE MIX (RECIPE, PAGE 59)
1/2 TEASPOON SAMBAL OELEK (HOT CHILI PASTE), OPTIONAL
1 TABLESPOON LEMON JUICE

1. Preheat the oven to 350 degrees.

2. Peel and quarter the red onion and place it in a shallow baking dish with the peeled garlic and shallot. Coat lightly with a Tablespoon of the olive oil and sprinkle with salt and pepper.

3. Roast in the center of the oven for 20 minutes.

4. Burn the skin of the bell pepper over an open flame and place in a plastic bag to steam for 3 minutes. Peel away the charred skin. Cut in half and remove the seeds and stem. Cut into 1/2-inch pieces.

5. When the onions, garlic and shallot are finished, place them in a blender with the remaining ingredients and 2 Tablespoons water, adding a little more water if necessary to produce a smooth sauce. Season with salt to taste.

*For this recipe, I have chosen a roasted pepper coulis to complement the delicate nature of the seafood. Seafood pâtés and terrines can be served with any number of sauces and accompaniments. A few other suggestions would be a sour cream-based sauce with herbs, such as dill or chives, a creamy mustard-flavored mayonnaise or aioli, or even a citrus butter sauce or beurre blanc if the pâté or terrine is to be served warm from the oven.* ▪

# COUNTRY-STYLE MUSHROOM PÂTÉ

2 TABLESPOONS UNSALTED BUTTER

1 1/2 CUPS CHOPPED YELLOW ONION

2 CUPS DICED WHITE BREAD, CRUSTS REMOVED

3/4 CUP HEAVY CREAM

3 TABLESPOONS PORT WINE

2 EGGS

2 TABLESPOONS UNSALTED BUTTER

4 CLOVES GARLIC, MINCED

2 POUNDS MIXED FRESH MUSHROOMS (PORTABELLA,
    SHIITAKE, OYSTER, TRUMPET, ETC.), 1/2-INCH DICE

2 TEASPOONS PÂTÉ SPICE (RECIPE, PAGE 213)

2 POUNDS PORK, COARSELY GROUND (FATTY PORK,
    LIKE PORK BUTT)

1/4 CUP CHOPPED FLAT LEAF PARSLEY

1/8 TEASPOON GROUND WHITE PEPPER

1/2 TEASPOON KOSHER SALT

8 SLICES "THICK SLICE" BACON (GET SPECIALTY SMOKED,
    LIKE APPLE-WOOD SMOKED, ETC.), OPTIONAL

4 SLICES WHOLE GRAIN BREAD

WHOLE GRAIN MUSTARD SAUCE (RECIPE FOLLOWS)

A FEW BABY GREENS FOR GARNISH

1. Heat a medium sauté pan over medium-high heat. Add the butter and then the onions. Cook, stirring frequently, until the onions start to turn brown. Remove the onions to a medium-sized mixing bowl and cool. Add the diced bread, heavy cream, port wine and eggs. Mix to combine.

2. Heat a large sauté pan over medium-high heat. Add the butter and garlic

*Fall mushroom harvests in Maine yield an abundant amount and variety of wild mushrooms. This pâté makes good use of the mushroom crop and is incredibly delicious. I also make this pâté with veal instead of pork. However, it is necessary to add additional pork fat since veal is rather lean.* ∎

and cook for 1 minute, stirring. Add the diced mushrooms and cook for 3 minutes, stirring. Sprinkle with the pâté spice and set aside to cool.

3. Place the ground pork in a large mixing bowl and add the onion mixture and combine well. Add the mushrooms, parsley and salt and pepper. Mix well to combine.

4. Preheat the oven to 350 degrees.

5. If you choose to use the bacon, line a small (5 cup) loaf pan with the sliced bacon by laying the bacon crosswise over the pan. Otherwise, just butter the loaf pan generously.

6. Fill the pan with the pâté mixture and smooth the top.

7. Fold the ends of the bacon over the top of the mixture, enclosing it neatly in bacon.

8. Place the pan in a shallow baking dish and fill with hot water, one inch up the sides. Bake in the center of the preheated oven for 1 hour. Remove and cool for 5 minutes. Invert the loaf pan over a bowl (to catch the juices) and release the pâté from the pan. Discard the juices.

9. The pâté can be made up to 4 days in advance and kept covered in the refrigerator until serving.

10. To serve, cut the whole grain bread with seasonal (snowflakes, fall leaves, flowers, hearts) cookie cutters and toast on each side. Slice the pâté into ¾-inch slices. Place a slice just off center on each plate and spoon a heaping Tablespoon of the whole grain mustard sauce on the exposed plate next to the pâté. Garnish the plates with a few baby greens and the toasted whole grain bread shapes.

## WHOLE GRAIN MUSTARD SAUCE

1 LARGE EGG YOLK
1 TEASPOON LEMON JUICE
2 TEASPOONS WHITE WINE VINEGAR
3/4 CUP CANOLA OIL
1/4 CUP WHOLE GRAIN MUSTARD
1 TEASPOON LIGHT BROWN SUGAR, FIRMLY PACKED
2 TEASPOONS CHOPPED CHIVES

1. Place the egg yolk in a medium-sized mixing bowl and whisk vigorously for 1 minute. Add the lemon juice, vinegar and 1 teaspoon of the mustard and continue whisking for another minute.

2. Add the oil to the bowl in a very slow stream while continuing to whisk vigorously. When the oil is completely incorporated, whisk in the remaining mustard, brown sugar and chives.

3. Keep covered and chilled until serving.

# Arts in the Park & Country Affairs

ARTS AND CRAFTS SHOWS, COUNTRY FAIRS, GARDEN TOURS AND HOUSE TOURS. Artists' studio tours, flea markets, antiques auctions and antiques fairs. Midcoast Maine has some of the best of each, and three that are considered destinations by almost anyone who lives in Maine are the HarborArts Juried Arts & Crafts Show, the Union Fair and the Common Ground Country Fair.

Held twice a year, always the third weekend in July and usually the first full weekend in October, the HarborArts Juried Arts & Crafts Show, which is just a short walk from the Inn, features more than 100 artists and craftspeople. Painters, glassblowers, weavers, photographers, jewelry makers, mixed media artists, sculptors, potters, and others display and sell their work in Harbor Park just above Camden's scenic waterfront. Music, sometimes "live," can be heard throughout the park. The atmosphere is one of friendly anticipation. The salt air is invigorating. The vendors' booths are all open air and their displays are both accessible and inviting. Strolling from one artist's wares to the next and then back again to something you found particularly compelling is half the fun. At the end of the weekend, you can't help but feel inspired.

The Union Fair, which runs for a full week in late August each year, is one of Maine's best agricultural fairs and is held at the Union fairgrounds, the backdrop of which is beautiful rolling hills. In existence since 1869, the Union Fair is extremely popular. The first day of the fair always lands on a Sunday and includes the coronation of the Wild Blueberry Festival queen. Daily musical entertainment, daily harness racing, midway rides and games, farm animal shows, various contests, and food galore are just a smattering of what this country fair offers. Every year, Friday is Wild Blueberry Festival day and all kinds of wild blueberry food items, including free individual blueberry pies, are available throughout the day. The Union Fair always ends on Saturday and culminates with the annual farm parade consisting of floats, marching bands, and farm animals decked out in the ribbons they won during the week.

The Common Ground Country Fair, always held the third weekend after Labor Day, takes place in Unity and is sponsored by the Maine Organic Farmers and Gardeners Association (MOFGA). Spread out over 35 acres, this unique, three-day country fair celebrates country living. There are herding demonstrations where you can watch border collies maneuver sheep into pens, workshops for stone cutting and carving, alternative energy booths, demonstrations for all levels of gardening, crafts tents, fibers and fleece for sale, and so much more. Drummers, jugglers and fiddlers meander the fairgrounds or perform on one of three stages for your enjoyment. And there's lots of food, almost all organic — Thai sweet chili noodles, sautéed shiitake mushrooms, lamb sausages, crab Rangoon, sorbet, ice cream, to name a few. No wonder this country fair is touted as a great place to find resources for everything organic and alternative.

Whether you're up for a cultural weekend experience or a casual, country affair, these are worth experiencing at least once in your lifetime. ■

# Haute Chinese

*I* WAS FIRST INTRODUCED TO THE PREPARATION OF CHINESE CUISINE at culinary school many years ago. The Chinese instructor made fun of our elaborate knife kits and commented that the only knife necessary in the kitchen was a cleaver. Later in my Hotel career I met a very talented Chinese chef, Mr. Chang at the Hyatt Regency in Lake Tahoe. I worked side by side with Mr. Chang in the kitchen and learned to really appreciate Chinese food at its finest.

Organization and advance preparation is the key to preparing Chinese food in a wok. Get all of your chopping, dicing, slicing and mincing done prior to any stove work. Traditionally, sauces are made in the wok as the last stage in the cooking process. I find it much easier to make the sauce in advance and add it to the finished product at the last moment. The cooking process goes so quickly in a wok and there is little opportunity to consult the recipe once you begin. To ensure the best results, I recommend arranging the ingredients next to the cooking area in the order they will be used. Read the recipe thoroughly and feel comfortable about the various steps involved during the cooking process prior to heating your wok.

I love good Chinese food, but it can be difficult to find. Often it is prepared with the cheapest of ingredients to make it more cost effective and less expensive on the menu. These recipes take common Chinese dishes and elevate them to a higher "haute" level as Mr. Chang did. If you are preparing for a party of 6 to 8 people, choose 2 dishes and serve them on platters family style with a double batch of steamed rice.

A WOK: Using the right wok is so important to the correct preparation of these dishes that I highly recommend you get one if you are at all serious about preparing Asian foods at home. Avoid electric woks, they don't get hot enough and you end up steaming your ingredients. Thin steel woks are preferable because they heat up so fast. Use a round bottom wok (and wok ring) on a gas stove, and a flat bottom wok on an electric range. A new wok will need to be cleaned and seasoned.

TO CLEAN YOUR WOK: Most steel woks come with a special coating that prevents "pre-consumer" rusting. To remove this coating, fill the wok with water and add 2 Tablespoons baking soda. Boil for about 15 minutes and pour out the water. Scrub well with a steel wool pad (Brillo) to remove the coating.

TO SEASON YOUR WOK: Now the wok needs to be seasoned, which prepares the pan for cooking. Dry the cleaned wok well and place over medium-high heat. When the pan gets very hot, add 1 teaspoon peanut oil or canola oil and use a paper towel (and metal tongs) to rub the oil over the entire inside surface. Repeat 2 more times with oil and paper towels and remove the pan from the heat. Take dry paper towels and rub the surface to remove any remaining oil and cool. The wok is now ready to use.

MAINTAINING YOUR WOK: With continued use, a steel wok will develop a black coating (which is desirable), so it is important to no longer use a scouring pad on the surface. Wash in hot water with a sponge and detergent, and dry it well. Place the pan back on the heat to ensure dryness (a wet pan will rust) and rub with a little oil and a paper towel. Store your wok in a place where moisture will not come in contact with it.

# UNG PAO SHRIMP

SERVES 4

1 1/2 POUNDS LARGE SHRIMP, PEELED AND DEVEINED
(16-20 COUNT)

## MARINADE

1 TEASPOON MINCED FRESH GINGER
1 TEASPOON MINCED GARLIC
2 TABLESPOONS CORNSTARCH
1 TABLESPOON GRANULATED SUGAR
1/4 TEASPOON FRESHLY GROUND BLACK PEPPER
1/2 TEASPOON KOSHER SALT

## SAUCE

1 CUP CHICKEN STOCK
1 TABLESPOON SAMBAL OELEK (HOT CHILI PASTE)
(USE HALF AS MUCH IF YOU LIKE IT MILD,
AND TWICE AS MUCH IF YOU LIKE FIRE)
1 TABLESPOON HOISIN SAUCE
1 TABLESPOON SESAME OIL
1/4 CUP SOY SAUCE
1 TEASPOON GINGER
1/2 TEASPOON GARLIC
2 TEASPOONS GRANULATED SUGAR
2 TEASPOONS CORNSTARCH
4 TEASPOONS DRY SHERRY

*Kung Pao is a classic dish from the Sichuan Province of China, known for its use of hot chilies in its cuisine. Chicken, beef or pork can also be used in place of the shrimp in this recipe, and the amount of heat can be adjusted by the quantity of sambal oelek (hot chili paste) used. The heat of the chilies, the sweetness of the sauce and the crunch of the peanuts make this a favorite dish.* ■

## THE REST

7 TABLESPOONS PEANUT OIL OR CANOLA OIL
1 CUP DICED YELLOW ONIONS, 1-INCH PIECES
2 CUPS QUARTERED BUTTON MUSHROOMS
1 CUP SHIITAKE MUSHROOM CAPS, SMALL ONES HALVED
    AND LARGE ONES QUARTERED
1 CUP DICED RED BELL PEPPER, 1-INCH PIECES
1 CUP BABY CORN, HALVED LENGTHWISE
1 CUP SLICED WATER CHESTNUTS
1/2 CUP UNSALTED AND ROASTED PEANUTS, TOASTED
2 TABLESPOONS GREEN ONIONS, GREEN PARTS ONLY,
    SLICED FINELY ON A BIAS

1. Remove all the shells and tail fins from the shrimp and combine in a bowl with all of the marinade ingredients. Mix together well and set in the refrigerator, covered, for 1 hour.

2. To make the sauce, combine all of the ingredients (except for the cornstarch and sherry) in a small saucepan. Set the pan over medium heat and bring to a boil. In a very small bowl, mix together the cornstarch and sherry until smooth. When the sauce comes to a boil, whisk in the cornstarch mixture (slurry) and reduce the heat to low. Simmer on low heat, stirring occasionally, for 4 minutes. Remove from the heat, cover and reserve.

3. Just before serving, heat a wok over high heat. Place 2 Tablespoons peanut oil or canola oil in the wok and add half of the marinated shrimp. Cook the shrimp, stirring every 15 seconds, for about 3 minutes. Remove the shrimp to a dish and repeat with 2 Tablespoons of oil and the remaining shrimp. Cook the same way and remove the shrimp to the plate with the other shrimp.

4. Place 3 Tablespoons of oil in the wok and add the onions. Cook the onions for 1 minute and add all the mushrooms. Cook for 2 minutes and add the bell

peppers, baby corn and water chestnuts. Cook for 1 minute and add half of the peanuts, the shrimp and the sauce. Heat through and serve with the steamed rice (recipe, page 239). Sprinkle with the remaining peanuts and green onions.

# $\mathscr{S}$WEET AND SOUR PORK

### SERVES 4

1 1/2 POUNDS PORK TENDERLOIN,
    TRIMMED OF FAT AND SILVER SKIN

## BATTER

1/2 CUP ALL-PURPOSE FLOUR
1/2 CUP CORNSTARCH
1 TEASPOON KOSHER SALT
2 TABLESPOONS CANOLA OIL
1 TABLESPOON DRY WHITE WINE
3/4 CUP COLD WATER

## SAUCE

1 CUP WHITE WINE VINEGAR
2/3 CUP KETCHUP
2/3 CUP GRANULATED SUGAR
2 TEASPOONS KOSHER SALT
1/3 CUP WATER
1/4 TEASPOON RED FOOD COLOR

## THE REST

2 CUPS, PLUS 2 TABLESPOONS PEANUT OIL OR CANOLA OIL
1 MEDIUM-SIZED CARROT, PEELED
1/2 CUP DICED YELLOW ONIONS, 1-INCH PIECES
4 GREEN ONIONS, CUT INTO 1-INCH PIECES

1/2 CUP DICED RED BELL PEPPER, 1-INCH PIECES
1 CUP DICED FRESH PINEAPPLE, 1/2-INCH CUBES
1 CUP SEEDLESS RED GRAPES, WITH STEMS REMOVED
1 CUP FRESH STRAWBERRIES, HALVED, WITH STEMS REMOVED

## Wine Notes

*Similar to shiraz, red zinfandel offers the same level of fruit and spice but leans more toward cherry and blackberry flavors as well as undertones of clove and garrigue. Cline Ancient Vines zinfandel shows all of these flavors and will pair well with both aspects of this dish. ■*

1. Cut pork tenderloin into ¾-inch cubes.

2. To make the batter, combine all of the ingredients in a medium-sized bowl and whisk together until smooth. Reserve.

3. Combine all of the sauce ingredients together in another bowl and whisk well. Reserve.

4. Remove the ends from the peeled carrot and slice thinly (⅛ inch) lengthwise. Place the strips on a cutting board and cut the strips on the bias into about ¾-inch pieces.

5. An hour before serving, heat the 2 cups of peanut oil or canola oil in the wok, set over medium-high heat. Add the cubed pork to the batter and mix in gently to coat. When the oil is hot, drop about 15 pieces of the pork cubes individually into the oil. Stir briefly with a metal spoon to separate the individual pieces and cook for about 4 minutes, until lightly golden. Remove the pork to a baking sheet lined with paper towels and repeat with the remaining pork, allowing the oil to reheat for 2 minutes between batches. Remove the oil from the wok (strain, cool and refrigerate the oil to use again for deep-fat frying in the next few months), and wipe the wok clean with a paper towel.

6. Just before serving, place the wok over medium-high heat and pour in the 2 Tablespoons of oil. Add the carrots to the wok and cook for 1 minute. Add the onions and scallions and cook for 1 minute. Add the peppers and cook, stirring for 30 seconds. Add the pork and fruit to the wok and stir, cooking for 1 minute. Add the sauce and cook for 2 minutes, stirring. Serve over steamed rice (recipe, page 239).

# CASHEW CHICKEN

### SERVES 4

2 POUNDS BONELESS AND SKINLESS CHICKEN BREASTS,
TRIMMED OF FAT AND CARTILAGE

## MARINADE

1 CHICKEN BOUILLON CUBE (KNORR, EXTRA-LARGE CUBES)
2 TEASPOONS DRY SHERRY
1/3 CUP CORNSTARCH

## SAUCE

1 CUP CHICKEN STOCK
2 TABLESPOONS DRY WHITE WINE
4 TABLESPOONS MUSHROOM SOY SAUCE
1 TABLESPOON GRANULATED SUGAR
1 TEASPOON SESAME OIL
2 TEASPOONS MINCED FRESH GINGER
1 TABLESPOON CORNSTARCH
2 TABLESPOONS RICE WINE VINEGAR

## THE REST

2 CUPS, PLUS 2 TABLESPOONS PEANUT OIL OR CANOLA OIL
2 CUPS QUARTERED BUTTON MUSHROOMS
1 1/2 CUPS CELERY PIECES, CUT ON BIAS INTO 1/2-INCH PIECES
1 CUP DICED RED BELL PEPPER, 1-INCH PIECES
1/2 CUP GREEN ONIONS, CUT IN 1-INCH LONG PIECES
    (GREENS ONLY)
1 CUP STRAW MUSHROOMS, DRAINED (ONE 15-OUNCE CAN)
1 CUP UNSALTED CASHEWS, TOASTED

*My variation of cashew chicken uses a mushroom soy sauce (available in Oriental markets) in the preparation of the sauce. I find this really complements the mushrooms used in the dish. Traditional recipes for cashew chicken use plain bottled oyster sauce. Unsalted "raw" cashews are available at health food stores (they are actually cooked but not roasted), but regular roasted and salted cashews can be rinsed of their salt and toasted if the unsalted version is not available. ■*

1. Cut the chicken breasts into ¾-inch pieces and place in a medium-sized bowl.

2. Mash the bouillon cube and the sherry together with the back of a Tablespoon, breaking the cube into tiny pieces. Add to the diced chicken breasts along with the cornstarch, mix well and reserve in the refrigerator.

3. To make the sauce, combine all of the ingredients (except for the cornstarch and rice wine vinegar) in a small saucepan. Set the pan over medium heat and bring to a boil. In a very small bowl, mix together the cornstarch and rice wine vinegar until smooth. When the sauce comes to a boil, whisk in the cornstarch mixture (slurry) and reduce the heat to low. Simmer on low heat, stirring occasionally for 4 minutes. Remove from the heat, cover and reserve.

4. An hour before serving, heat the 2 cups of peanut oil or canola oil in the wok, set over medium-high heat. When the oil is hot, drop about 20 pieces of the chicken cubes individually into the oil. Stir briefly with a metal spoon to separate the individual pieces and cook for about 2 minutes. Remove the chicken to a baking sheet lined with paper towels and repeat with the remaining chicken, allowing the oil to reheat for 2 minutes between batches. Remove the oil from the wok (strain, cool and refrigerate the oil to use again for deep-fat frying in the next few months), and wipe the wok clean with a paper towel.

5. Just before serving, place the wok over medium-high heat and pour in the 2 Tablespoons of oil. Add the button mushrooms and celery to the wok, and cook for 2 minutes, stirring. Add the red bell pepper and green onions and cook, stirring, for 1 minute. Stir in the straw mushrooms and the chicken and cook for 1 minute. Add the sauce and half of the cashews and cook for 1 minute, stirring. Serve over steamed rice (recipe, page 239) with the remaining cashews sprinkled on top.

## Wine Notes

*Chinese cuisine will offer clear and dominant flavors, the wines that are paired with them require the same discipline. For this reason, Australian shiraz works quite well with these types of dishes. The rich, jammy fruit and signature spiciness of the grape are the perfect foil to unique flavor and heat of this cuisine.* ■

# CRISPY WHOLE FISH WITH SPICY VEGETABLES AND SALTED BLACK BEANS

SERVES 4

4 WHOLE FIRM WHITE-FLESHED FISH (SNAPPER, SEA BASS),
  ABOUT 1 POUND EACH — IF YOU CAN'T GET WHOLE FISH,
  FILLET OF FISH (SNAPPER, HADDOCK, SEA BASS) WILL WORK,
  ABOUT 3 POUNDS

MARINADE

1 TEASPOON MINCED FRESH GINGER
1/4 CUP SOY SAUCE
2 TABLESPOONS DRY SHERRY
1 TABLESPOON CHINESE FIVE SPICE POWDER
1 TABLESPOON MINCED GREEN ONIONS

## SAUCE

- 1/4 CUP SALTED BLACK BEANS
- 2 TEASPOONS CORNSTARCH
- 2 TABLESPOONS RICE WINE VINEGAR
- 1 CUP CHICKEN STOCK
- 2 TEASPOONS HOT CHILI PASTE
  (SAMBAL OELEK)
- 1 1/4 TEASPOONS MINCED FRESH GINGER
- 1 TEASPOON GRANULATED SUGAR
- 2 TABLESPOONS OYSTER SAUCE
- 2 TABLESPOONS SOY SAUCE
- 1/4 CUP WHITE WINE

## THE REST

- 1/4 CUP CORNSTARCH
- 2 CUPS CANOLA OIL FOR FRYING
- 1 MEDIUM CARROT, JULIENNED
- 1/4 CUP JULIENNED FRESH GINGER
- 1 TABLESPOON MINCED GARLIC
- 1 RED BELL PEPPER, JULIENNED
- 1/2 CUP JULIENNED BAMBOO SHOOTS
- 5 GREEN ONIONS, GREEN PART ONLY,
  CUT INTO 1-INCH PIECES ON THE BIAS
- 3 PLUM TOMATOES, CORED, SEEDED AND DICED

*Mary Jo has always been a big fan of this dish. Some people can't get past the fact that the fish is staring back at them while they eat. Whole, appropriately sized fish can also be difficult to find. In either case, fish fillets work equally well in this recipe, and it is a whole lot easier to eat. ■*

1. Clean the fish by washing it thoroughly inside and out. Scale the fish with either a fish scaler or the back of a large knife, removing all of the scales. Leave the head on the fish but remove all of the fins with either a sharp pair of kitchen shears or a sharp knife.

## Wine Notes

*Riesling is the most common*

*choice with most Asian cuisine.*

*It offers a wide range of flavors*

*and the off-dry fruit character*

*of the grape melds nicely with*

*the array of spices used in most*

*dishes. Look for dry rieslings*

*from California or Washington*

*State or Kabinett and Spatlese*

*from Germany.* ■

2. Slash the flesh of the fish a few times on the diagonal to allow the marinade to penetrate into the fish. Mix together the ginger, soy, sherry, Chinese five spice and minced green onions. Spread onto both sides of the fish and marinate for 1 hour. Turn the fish over and marinate on the other side for 1 hour.

3. For the sauce, soak the salted black beans in 1 cup of cold water for 15 minutes. Pour into a strainer and rinse under running water for 10 seconds. Drain off all water. In a small bowl, mix together the 2 teaspoons cornstarch and 1 teaspoon of the rice wine vinegar. Combine the chicken stock, chili paste, ginger, remaining rice wine vinegar, sugar, oyster sauce, soy sauce and white wine in a small saucepan over medium-high heat. Bring to a boil and mix in the cornstarch mixture (slurry), whisking constantly until thickened. Reduce heat to low and cook for 2 minutes. Add the beans and reserve in a warm place.

4. Just before serving, drain the excess marinade from the fish and dust each side (of each fish) with the cornstarch. Heat 2 cups of canola oil in a wok set over medium-high heat until it is hot. A drop of water should dance when it hits the surface of the hot oil. Fry the whole fish one at a time for about 4 minutes per side. Drain the fish on paper towels. Keep warm in a preheated 250-degree oven while you finish frying the remaining fish. Fillets will cook in about 4 minutes (2 minutes per side), depending on their thickness.

5. When the fish is done, pour off all but 2 Tablespoons of the oil in the wok. Clean out any debris in the wok and add the carrots. Cook for 15 seconds, add the garlic and ginger and cook for 15 more seconds. Add the bell pepper, bamboo shoots, green onions and tomatoes and cook for 30 seconds. Add the sauce and heat through. Place the crisp fish on the serving plates and cover with the vegetable and sauce mixture. Serve immediately with steamed rice (recipe follows).

#  TEAMED RICE

SERVES 4

2 CUPS JASMINE RICE
2 CUPS COLD WATER
1 TEASPOON KOSHER SALT

1. Rinse the rice well and drain. Find a bowl that is large enough to hold 2 quarts of water and can also fit into a large (9-quart) stockpot.

2. Place 1 quart of water in the stockpot along with something to keep the bowl off the bottom of the pot, e.g., a steamer rack, bunched aluminum foil, ramekins.

3. Transfer the rice to the 2-quart bowl and add the salt and cold water. Place the bowl on top of the "steamer rack" in the pot and place the pot over high heat. Cover the pot and bring the water to a boil. At the boil, reduce the heat to medium and continue steaming the rice for 25 minutes.

4. Remove the bowl from the pot with a pair of tongs (be careful of the steam) and fluff the rice with a fork. Keep covered with plastic until serving. The steamed rice will remain hot for up to 1 hour if kept in a warm place.

*H*

*My recipe for steamed rice produces nice, fluffy rice utilizing equipment that is common in most kitchens. To simplify the job, I recommend that you invest in a rice cooker to achieve perfect rice every time without any hassle.* ■

## *Art Hopping*

HANDBLOWN GLASS. Classic automobiles. Sculpture. Handcrafted furniture. Photography. These and more reside in midcoast Maine's rich selection of museums and galleries.

The Farnsworth Art Museum & Wyeth Center, located on Main Street in downtown Rockland and no more than ten minutes from downtown Camden, houses a fine collection of 18th- and 19th-century American art by Frank Benson, Thomas Eakins, Eastman Johnson, and Gilbert Stuart, to name a few. In addition, the museum offers four new galleries devoted to contemporary art and a vast collection of works by 20th-century sculptor Louise Nevelson. Throughout each year, the Farnsworth provides a wide range of exhibitions and accompanying films, lectures and activities. The Wyeth Center, a renovated church built in the 1870s with details characteristic of a Shaker meetinghouse, and located across the street from the Farnsworth, offers two floors of galleries devoted to the work of three generations of Wyeths in Maine — N.C. Wyeth, Andrew Wyeth and James Wyeth. Practically surrounding the Farnsworth on the side streets and along Main Street you will find an array of galleries devoted to original works of art in almost every medium.

Owl's Head is the place to go if one of your interests lies in pioneer aircraft, historic automobiles, vintage bicycles, classic motorcycles, carriages and engines. The Owl's Head Transportation Museum celebrates transportation history and is located just three miles south of Rockland. It houses one of the best collections of pioneer aircraft and automobiles in the world. Replicas, originals and prototypes await your viewing. Each year, the museum also offers a wide selection of special events, from the annual New England auto auction to engine room demonstrations to antique aeroplane shows.

In downtown Rockport, literally five minutes from downtown Camden, the Center for Maine Contemporary Art, an airy and bright three floors of gallery space, offers year-round exhibitions of both traditional and nontraditional artwork by well-known Maine artists as well as emerging artists. The Center also provides a varied schedule of art-related lectures and discussions. In addition, the Rockport area offers galleries devoted

to one-of-a-kind works of fine art, mixed media, sculpture, photography, American handblown glass and handcrafted furniture.

Just steps from the center of Camden, one can also find lovely galleries on Elm Street and Bayview Street. You don't have to go any further than downtown Camden to enjoy outstanding galleries that provide a remarkable collection of contemporary folk sculpture, fine art, photography, original prints, watercolors and mixed media.

If art hopping is your thing, doing it in and around Camden, Maine, is nothing less than richly satisfying. It's a perfect way to discover the abundance of remarkable art and design located right here in midcoast Maine. ■

# Hors d'Oeuvres

*I*NEVITABLY, we all end up with the task of making hors d'oeuvres. Whether we are making them for our own dinner parties or taking them over to homes of friends or family, it often happens that the same hors d'oeuvres appear time and time again. We become efficient and confident with certain preparations and when the feedback is positive, it becomes even easier to prepare the same items. So here is a chance to mix things up a little bit. I have assembled a group of 9 hors d'oeuvre recipes with varied preparations and ingredients, which will give you some variety the next time you are required to prepare hors d'oeuvres. For planning purposes, a set of 5 hors d'oeuvre recipes from this section will easily feed a party of 12 people, with an average of 9 pieces per person. If you are planning a smaller party, cut recipes in half or choose a few favorites to highlight.

## SMOKED SALMON BARQUETTES

### YIELDS 12 PIECES

1 BATCH PASTRY DOUGH (RECIPE FOLLOWS)
NONSTICK VEGETABLE SPRAY
7 OUNCES SLICED SMOKED SALMON,
    RESERVING 2 OUNCES FOR GARNISH
1/4 CUP MINCED RED ONION
2 TABLESPOONS CAPERS
1 HARD-BOILED EGG, CHOPPED FINELY
3 SCALLIONS, GREEN PART ONLY, FINELY SLICED
2 TABLESPOONS CHOPPED FRESH DILL
1/4 CUP SOUR CREAM
1 TABLESPOON WHOLE GRAIN MUSTARD
2 TEASPOONS LEMON JUICE
1/4 TEASPOON GROUND BLACK PEPPER
FRESH DILL SPRIGS FOR GARNISH
CAVIAR FOR GARNISH (OPTIONAL)

*Barquettes are wonderful boat-shaped molds that add a bit of elegance to a tartlet that would otherwise be round. Available at most kitchen shops, the nonstick-coated molds work the best if you can find them. For the adventurous, I cold-smoke my own salmon here at the Inn and describe the process in the Smoking chapter of this cookbook. Otherwise, a good quality store-bought brand will do the job nicely.* ■

*Burgundy's Volnay and*

*Pommard appellations offer*

*pinot noirs that not only show*

*the grape's strawberry fruit*

*but also give off a smoky*

*almost gunflint aroma. They*

*are perfect for any smoked*

*dish, but are especially good*

*with the richness of salmon.*

*Bouchard and Louis Latour*

*are generally available but look*

*for offerings from Jean Marc*

*Bouley as well.* ■

1. Roll the chilled pastry dough out on a lightly floured surface until it is an ⅛-inch-thick rectangle. Spray 12 five-inch barquette (boat-shaped) molds lightly with nonstick vegetable spray and arrange them on the table to form a similar-sized rectangular area. Drape the pastry gently over all of the molds and roll over the top with a rolling pin, cutting the dough into the forms. Gently press the dough into the molds.

2. Line the filled shells with a small piece of parchment paper and fill with pie weights or dried beans. Bake in a 350-degree oven for 15 minutes, or until the shells begin to brown lightly. Carefully remove the weights/beans and parchment and bake for another 10 minutes. Cool on a rack for at least 10 minutes before removing the pastry from the molds. Cool completely.

3. Finely chop 5 ounces of the smoked salmon and place in a medium-sized mixing bowl with the minced red onion, capers, chopped egg, sliced scallions, chopped dill, sour cream, whole grain mustard, lemon juice and black pepper. Mix to combine.

4. Fill the chilled barquette molds with a teaspoon of the smoked salmon filling and cover the top with a small slice of smoked salmon. Garnish the top with a small sprig of fresh dill and a dab of caviar, if desired.

## PASTRY DOUGH

1⅓ CUPS ALL-PURPOSE FLOUR
3/4 TEASPOON KOSHER SALT
4 TABLESPOONS CHILLED, UNSALTED BUTTER
⅓ CUP VEGETABLE SHORTENING
1/4 CUP COLD WATER

1. In a mixer, combine the flour and salt. Cut the butter into fine cubes and mix into the flour until it resembles a fine meal. Add the shortening and mix for

30 seconds. Add the water and mix only until it combines. Do not overwork. Remove from the mixer and wrap in plastic wrap.

2. Refrigerate for at least 2 hours.

## FUNCHI ROUNDS WITH GRILLED TIGER SHRIMP AND SPICY LEMON AIOLI

YIELDS 24 PIECES

2 CUPS WATER
1/2 CUP YELLOW CORNMEAL
1/2 TEASPOON KOSHER SALT
1/4 CUP GRATED GRUYERE CHEESE
12 LARGE (16-20 COUNT)
    SHRIMP, PEELED AND DEVEINED
EXTRA VIRGIN OLIVE OIL
1/4 TEASPOON KOSHER SALT
1/4 TEASPOON GROUND
    FENNEL
1/8 TEASPOON FRESHLY GROUND
    BLACK PEPPER
1/8 TEASPOON GRANULATED
    GARLIC
2 TEASPOONS COARSELY CHOPPED
    ITALIAN PARSLEY
SPICY LEMON AIOLI
    (RECIPE FOLLOWS)

1. Combine 1/2 cup of water with the cornmeal and salt.

Wine Notes

The stunning region of Alsace, located along the eastern border of France, produces rieslings of unique character. They are some of the driest of all rieslings, while still maintaining the desired fruit flavors. Trimbach is one of the standard bearers of the appellation and the Cuvee Fredrick Emile will bring forth the flavor of the shrimp without lessening that of the cheese or aioli. ■

2. Boil the remaining 1½ cups of water over high heat. At a boil, whisk the softened cornmeal into the water, stirring constantly until thickened. Stir in the gruyere cheese. Cover and reduce the heat to low, continuing to cook for 5 minutes.

3. For this recipe I use two mini muffin pans. Each pan has 12 small, round hollows. Place an oversized piece of plastic wrap over each muffin pan. Starting at one end, fill each plastic-lined hollow with a heaping Tablespoon of the hot cornmeal mix. Press the mixture into the hollow, forming a firm cake. Using your thumb, create a small indentation in the top of each cornmeal round. Refrigerate until set, about 20 minutes.

4. Combine the shrimp with the olive oil, salt and spices. Mix well to combine. Heat a grill pan over high heat and grill the shrimp, for 2 minutes on each side (just barely cook through, or they will be dry). Slice the shrimp in half lengthwise creating 2 equal halves.

5. Un-mold the cornmeal rounds and fill the indentation with a dollop of the spicy lemon aioli. Top with a grilled shrimp half and a sprinkle of Italian parsley.

## SPICY LEMON AIOLI

4 GARLIC CLOVES
2 LARGE EGG YOLKS
2 TABLESPOONS FRESH LEMON JUICE
1 TEASPOON SWEET PAPRIKA
1/4 TEASPOON CAYENNE PEPPER
1 TEASPOON DIJON MUSTARD
1/2 CUP EXTRA VIRGIN OLIVE OIL
1/3 CUP CANOLA OIL
KOSHER SALT TO TASTE

1. Mince the garlic and mash it with the side of a large knife (using a little salt) until it becomes a smooth paste. In a small mixing bowl, whisk together the egg yolks, lemon juice, paprika, cayenne and Dijon mustard.

2. While whisking the egg mixture vigorously, add the oils in a very slow stream. Whisk constantly, adding the oil slowly until all of the oil is incorporated. Add the mashed garlic and season with salt. Cover and chill.

## Goat Cheese and Pine Nut Tarts

### YIELDS 18 PIECES

1 PACKAGE FROZEN PUFF PASTRY DOUGH
1 EGG
8-OUNCE GOAT CHEESE LOG — PREFERABLY
    1½-INCH-ROUND LOGS
1 OUNCE PINE NUTS
KOSHER SALT
SUN-DRIED TOMATO TAPENADE (RECIPE FOLLOWS)
1 TEASPOON CHOPPED FLAT LEAF PARSLEY FOR GARNISH

1. Preheat an oven to 350 degrees. Spray a baking sheet with nonstick vegetable spray.

2. Thaw the puff pastry and use a 2-inch scalloped round cookie cutter to cut 18 circles of dough. Spread out on the prepared baking sheet. Break the egg into a small bowl and whisk briefly with a fork. Brush the pastry circles with a little egg wash to coat.

3. Cut the goat cheese into eighteen ⅜-inch slices. If using larger pieces of goat cheese, form the cheese into 1½-inch logs and slice into ⅜-inch slices. Place

*These tarts are very simple and quick to make. I use goat cheese from a local artisan at Appleton Creamery for this hors d'oeuvre, but any good quality goat cheese will work. If you would like to save time, buy a premade tapenade and use it as is or add some finely chopped sun-dried tomatoes to it. They are best if served warm.* ■

*Goat cheese and New Zealand*

*sauvignon blanc is one of the*

*great pairings in all the wine*

*world. Both are intense in*

*flavor and show a lingering*

*acidity. Alone they can be*

*addictive or off-putting,*

*depending on your point of*

*view. When combined,*

*however, the acid in one is*

*offset by the other, and what*

*is left is the sweet cream of*

*the cheese and the brilliant*

*fruit of the wine. Truly a*

*match not to be missed.* ∎

the goat cheese in the center of the puff pastry circles. Sprinkle the tarts with pine nuts (some on the goat cheese and some on the exposed dough) and follow the pine nuts with a sprinkling of kosher salt.

4. Bake in a preheated 350-degree oven for 35 minutes, or until they turn golden brown.

5. Top the tarts with a teaspoon of the sun-dried tomato tapenade and sprinkle with the chopped parsley.

## SUN-DRIED TOMATO TAPENADE

1/2 CUP PITTED KALAMATA OLIVES
1/4 CUP SUN-DRIED TOMATOES
1 SMALL GARLIC CLOVE, MINCED
1 ANCHOVY FILLET
1 1/2 TEASPOONS CAPERS
2 TABLESPOONS EXTRA VIRGIN OLIVE OIL

1. Place all of the ingredients in a food processor and blend to a fine paste.

# Spicy Beef Toasts with a Smoked Tomato Confit

YIELDS 20 PIECES

10 ounces beef tenderloin steak (tail end)

Extra virgin olive oil

Cajun Spice Mix (recipe follows)

1 thin French baguette

Smoked Tomato Confit (recipe, page 286)

20 oil-cured olives (pitted) for garnish

Chive batons for garnish (³/4-inch pieces)

*Tomatoes add a certain acidity*

*to this dish, and the wines of*

*Tuscany will lessen that aspect*

*and bring out the true quality*

*of the fruit. In this case, a*

*simple sangiovese or rosso*

*di Montalcino will provide*

*the black cherry fruit, light*

*toastiness and clean acidity*

*to highlight both the meat*

*and spice.* ■

1. Place the beef on a plate and drizzle with some olive oil. Roll the meat around to coat it well. Generously sprinkle Cajun spice mix over the steak, coating it well. Marinate for 1 hour.

2. With a serrated knife, slice the baguette into twenty ½-inch-thick slices. Place in a covered bowl and reserve.

3. Heat a medium-sized sauté pan over medium-high heat. When hot, add a splash of olive oil and sear the beef for 1 minute per side, turning the meat to sear it all over. Transfer to a preheated 350-degree oven for about 5 minutes depending on thickness. Meat should be cooked to medium-rare. Let the meat rest for 5 minutes before slicing it.

4. Heat another large sauté pan over medium heat, add a thin layer of olive oil and toast the baguette rounds. Turn and toast the other side, adding a little more olive oil. Transfer the toasts to a serving platter and continue with the remaining bread.

5. Just before serving, slice the beef into 20 very thin slices and place on the toasted baguette. Top with a teaspoon of the smoked tomato confit and garnish with the cured olives and chives.

## CAJUN SPICE MIX

1/4 CUP KOSHER SALT

1/4 CUP GROUND SWEET PAPRIKA

3 TABLESPOONS GROUND CAYENNE PEPPER

2 TABLESPOONS FRESHLY GROUND BLACK PEPPER

2 TABLESPOONS DRIED THYME LEAVES

2 TABLESPOONS CELERY SEED

2 TABLESPOONS DRIED OREGANO

2 TABLESPOONS ONION POWDER

2 TABLESPOONS GARLIC POWDER

2 TABLESPOONS GRANULATED SUGAR
2 TEASPOONS DRIED BASIL
1 TEASPOON CHILI POWDER
1/2 TEASPOON GROUND CUMIN
1/2 TEASPOON GROUND CORIANDER

1. Mix all the spices and dried herbs together and keep in a covered jar.

# CHILLED WILD MUSHROOM TERRINE

## YIELDS ENOUGH FOR 12 PEOPLE

1 POUND VARIOUS MUSHROOMS (THE MORE VARIETY
   THE BETTER — CHANTERELLE, OYSTER, MORELS,
   SHIITAKE, PORTABELLA, ETC.)
1 TABLESPOON UNSALTED BUTTER
2 LARGE SHALLOTS, FINELY CHOPPED
1 LARGE GARLIC CLOVE, MINCED
1/4 CUP DRY SHERRY
1/4 TEASPOON KOSHER SALT
1/8 TEASPOON GROUND BLACK PEPPER
1/2 TEASPOON GROUND CARAWAY SEEDS
1/2 TEASPOON WHITE TRUFFLE OIL (OPTIONAL)
4 OUNCES CREAM CHEESE, ROOM TEMPERATURE
1 1/2 TEASPOONS CHOPPED FRESH CHIVES
1 1/2 TEASPOONS CHOPPED FRESH DILL
1 1/2 TEASPOONS CHOPPED FRESH BASIL

1. Wipe the mushrooms clean and coarsely chop them into ½-inch pieces.

2. Melt the butter in a large sauté pan over medium-high heat. Add the chopped shallots and cook for 2 minutes, stirring until softened. Add the garlic and

continue to cook for 30 seconds. Add the mushrooms and continue to cook, stirring, until the mushrooms are softened and start to brown.

3. Deglaze the pan with the sherry and add the salt, black pepper and caraway. Cook until the sherry is gone and the pan is dry. Set aside and cool to room temperature.

4. Place the cooled mushrooms in a food processor with the remaining ingredients. Pulse to combine, being careful not to over-puree. Transfer to a decorative terrine mold and refrigerate until firm, about 2 hours. (If you wish to serve unmolded, pre-line the terrine with plastic wrap.)

5. Serve the terrine chilled with toasted bread or crackers.

## Baked Brie with Hazelnuts and Frangelico

SERVES 6

1 MEDIUM WHEEL BRIE CHEESE (500 GM)
1/2 CUP UNSALTED BUTTER
1/2 CUP LIGHT BROWN SUGAR, FIRMLY PACKED
2 TABLESPOONS CUMIN SPICE MIX (RECIPE, PAGE 128)
1/2 CUP FRANGELICO (HAZELNUT LIQUEUR)
1/2 CUP HAZELNUTS, WHOLE
1 LOAF FRENCH BREAD

1. Preheat the oven to 350 degrees.

2. Place the Brie in an ovenproof baking dish.

3. In a small saucepan, combine the butter, brown sugar, cumin spice mix and

(RECIPE, PAGE 128)

*Wine Notes*

*While not a traditional match, the New World-style riojas from Spain show a wonderful dusty fruit character that pairs well with the creaminess of the Brie while maintaining enough depth to match the flavors of the hazelnuts.* ■

Frangelico. Melt over medium heat and pour over the Brie. Sprinkle with the hazelnuts and cover with foil. Bake for 30 minutes in the preheated oven.

4. Serve immediately with sliced French bread.

# PROSCIUTTO-WRAPPED JUMBO SHRIMP WITH MAYTAG BLUE CHEESE

YIELDS 24 PIECES

24 JUMBO SHRIMP, PEELED AND DEVEINED
FENNEL SPICE MIX (RECIPE, PAGE 59)
1/4 POUND MAYTAG BLUE CHEESE (OR OTHER
   GOOD QUALITY CREAMY BLUE CHEESE)
12 SLICES (ABOUT 1/4 POUND) PROSCIUTTO,
   SLICED A LITTLE THICKER THAN USUAL
2 CUPS BABY SPINACH LEAVES
EXTRA VIRGIN OLIVE OIL FOR SEARING
SPICY LEMON AIOLI (RECIPE, PAGE 248)

1. Remove all of the shell from the shrimp, leaving only the tail fin section attached. Also remove the sharp-pointed shell piece from the fin section. Shrimp have a natural curl to their shape, and in this dish we want to straighten them out. Place each shrimp on a cutting board (belly down) and gently press on the top of it. When flattened, butterfly the shrimp by cutting down from the top (the length of the shrimp), almost reaching the bottom, but not cutting through, and gently press the shrimp open. Continue to flatten and butterfly the remaining shrimp.

2. Sprinkle the shrimp with the fennel spice mix and place some of the blue

*Prosciutto is almost always best when it is sliced as thin as you can possibly get it, without it falling apart. This makes it quite tender when it is wrapped around a wedge of melon or served on the top of a frittata. For this dish, the prosciutto is sliced a little thicker to provide some structure to the stuffed shrimp during the searing process. Maytag is a creamy and flavorful blue cheese made in Newton, Iowa, since 1941.* ■

*The saltiness of this dish*

*requires something a little*

*different. Italy's sparkling*

*prosecco provides enough fruit*

*to show off the sweetness of the*

*prosciutto and enough acidity*

*to highlight the creaminess of*

*the Maytag blue. Carpene*

*Malvolti is one of the original*

*producers of the wine and*

*continues to make one of*

*the best.* ■

cheese in the butterflied shrimp, wrapping the sides up around the cheese. Slice the prosciutto slices in half lengthwise and lay a few leaves of the baby spinach on each slice. Place the stuffed shrimp on the narrow end of the prosciutto slice and roll each shrimp up with the spinach and prosciutto, leaving the tail fin exposed, and secure with a toothpick. Continue rolling the remaining shrimp.

3. Place a large sauté pan over medium heat. When it is hot, add the olive oil. Place the shrimp in the pan and cook, lightly browning the prosciutto, about 2 minutes per side or until the shrimp are cooked through. Remove the toothpicks. This dish can be served hot or at room temperature with the spicy lemon aioli on the side.

# Smoked Salmon Pinwheel Toasts

### YIELDS 32 PIECES

1 RIPE AVOCADO
1 TEASPOON LEMON JUICE
4 OUNCES CREAM CHEESE, ROOM TEMPERATURE
KOSHER SALT AND WHITE PEPPER TO TASTE
2 TABLESPOONS NONPAREIL CAPERS
8 OUNCES SMOKED SALMON, SLICED
1 LOAF SLICED WHOLE GRAIN BREAD
2 TABLESPOONS MAYONNAISE
A FEW LEAVES OF ROMAINE LETTUCE

1. Peel and seed the avocado and cut into ½-inch pieces. Place the avocado and lemon juice in the bowl of a food processor and blend until smooth. Add the cream cheese and blend until well combined. Season with salt and white pepper. Add the capers and mix in by hand.

2. Spread out a 2-foot-long piece of plastic wrap in front of you, with the long side closest to you. Lay half of the salmon out in a single layer forming a rectangle (8 inches wide by 6 inches deep), centering it on the front edge of the plastic nearest to you. Repeat with a second piece of plastic and the second half of the salmon.

3. Place half of the cream cheese mixture on each layer of smoked salmon and use an offset spatula to spread it out in an even layer on the front ¾ of the rectangle, leaving a strip of salmon exposed along the back edge. Gently begin to roll the salmon into a pinwheel, using the plastic wrap to assist in the rolling. When the roll is complete, move it to the front center edge of the plastic and roll it up tightly in the plastic, leaving a long end of plastic on each side. Pinch the excess plastic wrap near the salmon roll and tie a knot, moving it in tight against the salmon. Repeat on the other side, firming up the roll. Continue with the other roll. Place in the freezer for 2 hours, or until the rolls set up firm.

4. Cut the bread with a 2-inch scalloped round cutter and toast under the broiler on each side. Place a dollop of mayonnaise on each toast round and top with a small square of romaine lettuce.

5. Pull the salmon rolls out of the freezer to soften slightly (10 minutes) at room temperature. Slice the salmon pinwheel (⅜-inch slices) while mostly frozen leaving the plastic on as you slice. Try to get around 16 slices from each roll. Peel away the plastic and place the pinwheels on the prepared toasts. Serve once the salmon thaws, about 20 minutes, depending on room temperature.

*Wine Notes*

*Not often produced on its own, semillon is a great match for simply prepared salmon. Its floral quality and medium weight go well with the flavor and texture of the fish. Several Australian producers such as Loan Vineyards make wine from this varietal.* ▪

# Peking Duck with Scallion Pancakes

### YIELDS 24 PIECES

4 DUCK BREASTS (MAPLE LEAF FARMS IS A GREAT BRAND)
1 TEASPOON SESAME OIL
1 TEASPOON CHINESE FIVE SPICE POWDER
1 TEASPOON KOSHER SALT
HOISIN DUCK SAUCE (RECIPE FOLLOWS)
SCALLION PANCAKES (RECIPE FOLLOWS)
8 SCALLIONS, CUT INTO 2-INCH-THICK STRIPS

1. Preheat the oven to 350 degrees.

2. Trim any excess skin, fat and silver skin from the duck breasts. Rub the duck with sesame oil and season with the Chinese five spice powder and kosher salt.

3. Place a large sauté pan over high heat until it is very hot. Place the duck breasts in the pan, skin side down and reduce the heat to medium-high. Continue cooking for 5 minutes on the first side. Turn the breasts over and sear the second side for 5 minutes. Remove the duck to an ovenproof pan and place in the oven to finish cooking for 5 to 7 minutes.

4. Remove the duck from the oven and let stand 3 minutes to allow the juices to settle.

5. Slice the duck breast into thin slices. Lay a few duck slices, a dab of the hoisin duck sauce and scallion pieces in the scallion pancakes, and roll, securing with a toothpick if necessary. Serve with the hoisin duck sauce.

*Scallion pancakes take a little time to make, but they are fun and worth the effort. Unfortunately, there are no sufficient substitutes available. They get paper-thin by being rolled out in pairs, fried until they are just cooked through and are then peeled apart. These make a fine addition to any hors d'oeuvres spread.* ■

## HOISIN DUCK SAUCE

1/4 CUP HOISIN SAUCE
1/2 CUP CHICKEN OR DUCK STOCK
1/4 CUP DRY SHERRY
1 TABLESPOON SOY SAUCE
1 1/2 TEASPOONS SESAME OIL
1 1/2 TEASPOONS GRANULATED SUGAR
1 TEASPOON KOSHER SALT
1/2 TEASPOON GROUND SZECHUAN PEPPER
    (OR USE WHITE PEPPER)
1 1/2 TEASPOONS CORNSTARCH
1 TEASPOON COLD WATER

1. Place all of the ingredients (except for the cornstarch and water) in a small saucepan and bring to a boil.

2. Simmer for 5 minutes. In another small bowl, combine the cornstarch with the cold water to make a slurry. Whisk the slurry into the sauce to thicken it. Continue simmering for 2 minutes. Serve slightly warm.

## SCALLION PANCAKES

1 CUP, PLUS 2 TABLESPOONS ALL-PURPOSE FLOUR
1/2 CUP BOILING WATER
1 SCALLION, FINELY CHOPPED
SESAME OIL
CANOLA OIL FOR FRYING

1. Place the flour in a medium-sized bowl and stir in the boiling water.

2. Knead until smooth, about 5 minutes, and rest for 15 minutes.

*Wine Notes*

*Red Burgundy has always been the preferred choice for duck entrées. The vibrant strawberry and cherry fruit along with the hints of smoke, earth and spice play beautifully with the richness of the meat. Wines from Gevrey Chambertain or Vosne Romanee offer a more generous fruit than some other appellations, and accentuate the crisp flavors of the Peking duck.* ∎

3. Add the scallions to the dough and knead until well incorporated.

4. Cut the dough into small, dime-sized pieces and roll into balls. Using a rolling pin, roll the balls into ⅛-inch-thick disks. Brush one side of each disk with sesame oil and sandwich two disks together, oiled sides together. Roll each sandwiched disk out into an oval shape about 2 inches by 4 inches and very thin. Continue with all of the dough, stacking them on a plate and covering them with moist paper towels.

5. Heat a medium-sized sauté pan over medium-high heat. Add a touch of canola oil and fry the pancake until each side is lightly browned. Remove the pancake from the pan and peel the two halves apart, yielding two scallion pancakes. Continue with the remaining pancakes.

*H*

# Grand SURPRISE

A TWO-HOUR SAIL OUT OF CAMDEN HARBOR on the elegant *Surprise*, the oldest day sailing windjammer in Camden, lets you experience both Camden and Penobscot Bay in a truly special and memorable way. From Memorial Day to mid-October, first mate Barbara and her husband Captain Jack Moore offer four 2-hour day trips on the 57-foot, two-masted *Surprise*.

Only the seventh owners of *Surprise*, Barbara and Jack have been sailing 39 of their 42 years of marriage, the last 20 out of Camden Harbor on *Surprise*, the first fisherman yacht built in America and now listed on the National Historic Register.

During the 1800s, all along the New England coast, American schooners, used primarily for fishing and to carry cargo, were fast and beautiful under sail. Over time, they became faster, more beautiful and safer for those on board in large part because of Thomas F. McManus, a brilliant designer of fishing schooners. His designs caught the attention of Martin S. Katenhorn, a Wall Street merchandise broker who enjoyed racing sailboats. In the early 1900s, "Marty" commissioned Tom McManus to design a smaller version of a McManus fisherman schooner "with a fisherman's style of rig, with double headsails, gaff foresail, gaff mainsail and main topsail" specifically for racing and cruising. D.M. Waddell of Rockport, Massachusetts, built this exceptionally strong, fast and trim vessel, and, with much fanfare, *Surprise* was launched in 1918.

She hasn't missed a season of sailing since. *Surprise* lived in New Rochelle for forty-one years and has been in Camden, Maine, since 1986. She underwent renovations in the early 1980s, and during the winter of 2004–2005, underwent extensive renovations. As a consequence, she is healthier than she's been in 65 years.

———

The horn blasts once, which announces to all in the harbor that *Surprise* is leaving the Camden Public Landing, and three blasts announce that she's backing up. *Surprise* glides through the harbor past the occasional kayaker and *Lively Lady*, a lobster boat that offers lobster tours and island tours, all kinds of working and cruising boats, and past *When and If*, General George Patton's 1914 windjammer. Captain Jack steers with one

foot while he relaxes against the mainsail boom as *Surprise* moves out past Curtis Island and its quaint lighthouse and into the cold, clear waters of spectacular Penobscot Bay.

Jack laughs as he lets passengers know that he hates at-sea rescues so when he asks everyone to sit while the boom moves across the expanse of the boat he expects them to sit. Barbara shows everyone where the life jackets are stowed and where to find strategically placed binoculars.

As they prepare to raise the sails, they ask who wants to help. "We used to do it all ourselves, until we realized that some passengers have more fun participating," Barbara says.

"Ready about," Captain Jack calls out, and with a graceful turn of direction, they begin to tack by a pile of rocks known as "the graves" that had a lighthouse until 2001, when it was removed because the Coast Guard could no longer afford to maintain it. They sail by Goose Rock Island and East Goose Rock Island with many more islands in the

distance. Almost 4,000 islands exist in Maine, and those in Penobscot Bay make a stunning backdrop. Eventually, everyone settles back, including resident half tabby/half Siamese cat, Robbie, age 13. He's been on board since he was a kitten and loves the water almost as much as he likes to eat. For those who would like a snack, a basket of fruit and really good cookies is passed around.

When Barbara and Jack were first married, neither of them had ever been on a sailboat. "It was nice to fall in love with sailing together," Barbara says. It became a passion. Since their first sail, they have logged over 20,000 miles of cruising together. She had been an English teacher and he a science teacher and prior to owning *Surprise*, they lived on their ketch *Milky Way* for seven years with their four children who they educated on board. They visited ports from Nova Scotia to the Lesser Antilles.

After they decided to start a day sailing business, they researched areas from Newport north and when they happened on Camden their search came to a stop. Camden offered everything they were looking for: a lovely community that's nestled at the base of Camden Hills, which is a breathtaking sight from the bay; ease in and out of the harbor; protection in open water; a sweet spot for day sailing with sails up.

Barbara and Jack love to share the day and the sea and the area with their passengers. A professor from Bowdoin College rented *Surprise* for his parents' 63rd wedding anniversary. With the celebratory couple's extended family on board, they enjoyed a truly special event.

Recently, someone called to find out which boat would give him the best view of Camden. "That, of course, was impossible to answer," Barbara says, "because we all do." Three other day sails besides *Surprise* that operate out of Camden Harbor are *Olad*, *Lazy Jack II* and *Appledore*.

Barbara and Jack are very careful and are known in the harbor as the most conservative vessel, and that's the way they prefer it. They'd rather play it safe if a storm is brewing, and come in quick or cancel a trip before it breaks loose, rather than subject customers to high winds and lumpy seas with thunder, lightning and rain. Day sailing for their passengers is all about unwinding and feeling the wind on their faces as they tack past islands and just as often porpoise, seals, loons and osprey. With only 18 passengers maximum, cushioned seating for all, and a spacious amount of deck space, *Surprise* offers a tranquil and intimate experience.

During sailing season, Jack and Barbara live on their windjammer. They've been known to sail 30 to 35 days in a row, without a single day off. Do they mind? Not in the slightest. "Penobscot Bay and Camden is a beautiful area to share with people," says Barbara. That they can also share their splendid windjammer *Surprise* makes them feel fortunate indeed as it does those who have sailed her. As one passenger put it, "What an amazing surprise this was. I loved every minute of it." ◾

# Smoking Foods at Home

## SMOKING BASICS

*S*MOKING IS A GREAT WAY TO EXPAND YOUR COOKING REPERTOIRE and add a new level of interest and depth to your menus. In Maine, we have an abundance of fresh seafood that lends itself well to smoking. I smoke a great deal of salmon at the Inn and use it for breakfast, tea and dinner. Scallops, mussels and other types of shellfish transform into luscious nuggets of flavor when exposed to a light smoking from mild woods. Meats like pork and chicken are more traditional "smoker fare" and benefit from longer smoking times and exposure to more assertive woods such as hickory and mesquite. Once the basic principles of smoking are understood and you get a little practice under your belt, experiment with other meats and vegetables and create your own rubs and sauces.

The first time I offered a smoking cooking class at the Inn, the turnout was rather bleak. It seemed as though there was very little interest among my regular attendees in learning how to smoke foods at home. The few students who did attend thoroughly enjoyed the class and some have even purchased stovetop smokers for themselves. The initial investment in equipment is minimal and the results are fabulous. Make sure you have proper ventilation in your kitchen before attempting to smoke on your stove. I have found that the average residential kitchen vent will do the job nicely.

EQUIPMENT: For most of the recipes, we will be using a stovetop smoker by Camerons (the brand name), which is the only one that is widely available and very efficient. There are many types of backyard smokers that also work quite well if you decide to upgrade to a larger model, but the Camerons smoker is an inexpensive ($50) investment that works great.

HEAT: Gas and electric stoves both work well for the stovetop smoker, while flat-topped stoves are a little tricky and the manufacturer has some warnings about their use. A medium heat inside the smoker (between 350 and 375 degrees) is ideal for smoking.

WOOD: Stovetop smokers use finely shaved woods (available from the manufacturer) while other smokers use anything from small chips to very large chunks. In addition, several types of wood are used for smoking foods, depending on the levels of smoke intensity that they impart to the food. Some are milder while others are much more assertive. Fruit woods, for example, rather than imparting a "fruity" flavor, provide a flavor that is milder than that of hickory wood. Here is a basic chart of woods and their flavor intensities:

| INTENSITY LEVEL: | TYPE OF WOODS: |
| --- | --- |
| Mild Woodsy Flavor | Apple, Cherry and Alder |
| Medium Woodsy Flavor | Pecan, Maple and Oak |
| Assertive Woodsy Flavor | Hickory and Mesquite |

## SMOKED CHEESE

SMOKING CHEESE is a rather delicate matter because too much heat will melt the cheese. Use a delicate wood like apple so the smoky flavor doesn't overpower the cheese. Semisoft cheeses such as mozzarella, Gouda and cheddars all take on the flavor of the smoke well. Start this recipe with a cold smoker. Place the cheese on a lightly oiled rack and smoke for 10 minutes with 2 Tablespoons apple chips. Remove the pan from the heat, leaving the cover in place, and allow the smoke to be exposed to the cheese for another 10 minutes off the heat.

## SESAME-SMOKED NUTS

ALL TYPES OF NUTS will work in this recipe, but almonds work especially well. Toss a few cups of nuts with a teaspoon of sesame oil and one Tablespoon of the Sesame Spice Mixture (recipe follows). Smoke for about 15 minutes with 2 Tablespoons hickory chips or mesquite chips. Serve warm.

*Wine Notes*

*The creaminess of the semisoft cheeses suggested in this recipe usually call for a crisp white wine, but the smoke adds both depth and flavor to the cheese and, therefore, demands a more robust wine. King Estate pinot noir from Oregon has wonderful cherry fruit and just a hint of gunflint and smoke, and is just light enough to enhance rather than overpower the cheese.* ∎

*When a tawny port is aged for*

*twenty years, it takes on a rich*

*amber hue and the aromas of*

*caramel and roasted nuts reach*

*an almost decadent level. When*

*paired with these well-spiced*

*treats, it makes afternoon tea*

*just a bit more interesting.* ■

*Salmon and pinot noir are one*

*of the great food pairings. The*

*strawberry to cherry*

*flavors of the wine blunt the*

*more intense seafood quality,*

*while the light but firm tannins*

*of the wine soften the slightly*

*oily texture of the fish. When*

*salmon is served cold, look for*

*a lighter, fruitier pinot from*

*Oregon or New Zealand.* ■

### SESAME SPICE MIXTURE

1/4 CUP KOSHER SALT
2 TABLESPOONS WHITE SESAME SEEDS
1 1/2 TEASPOONS CAYENNE PEPPER
1/4 CUP POWDERED SUGAR

I. Place the kosher salt in a spice grinder with the sesame seeds and cayenne. Blend until well ground, about 1 minute. Mix together with the powdered sugar.

## SMOKING SALMON

WE SMOKE A LOT OF SALMON AT THE INN. Generally when I refer to smoked salmon, I am referring to cold-smoked salmon, which is a cured side of salmon that is gently smoked at low temperatures. With cold smoking, the salmon is "cooked" by the curing process and "flavored" by the smoke. The distinctive texture of cold-smoked salmon comes from curing, and makes the flesh firm but not crumbly like salmon exposed to heat. Hot-smoked salmon, on the other hand, is seasoned fresh salmon that is smoked at high temperatures (350 degrees) and the fish actually cooks through while smoking.

### DRY CURE MIX

1 CUP GRANULATED SUGAR
3/4 CUP KOSHER SALT
1 TABLESPOON DRIED DILL

I. Mix all of the ingredients together.

# COLD-SMOKED SALMON

COAT BOTH SIDES OF A ONE-POUND SALMON FILLET (skin on, pin bones removed) with ¼ cup of the Dry Cure Mix (recipe, opposite). Place the salmon in a small container with a lid and refrigerate for 24 hours. This process is known as "curing." The salt will draw out a great deal of liquid from the salmon and preserve it, actually "cooking" the flesh. After 24 hours, gently rinse both sides of the salmon under cold water and place skin side down on the smoking rack. Cold smoke the salmon (at a maximum of 90 degrees) for 2 hours with cherry chips. This is a delicate process in the stovetop smoker. The best technique is to get the smoker to the point where it is producing smoke, place the salmon on the smoking rack, close the cover and remove the pan from the heat. Allow the smoke to be exposed to the salmon for 10 minutes off the heat then remove the salmon from the pan and continue the process over and over for a full 2 hours. Add new cherry chips as necessary. Cold-smoked salmon is best if allowed to rest for 24 hours before slicing very thinly.

# HOT-SMOKED SALMON (OR OTHER FIRM-FLESHED FISH)

SQUEEZE A LITTLE FRESH LEMON JUICE over 6-ounce salmon fillets (skin off, pin bones removed) and lightly coat with a seasoning rub of your choice (see Rubs and Sauces section, page 284). Place them on the lightly oiled smoking rack and hot smoke at 350 degrees for 15 minutes with 2 Tablespoons apple, cherry or alder chips. Serve with a fruit salsa, herbed sour cream, mustard or Chimi Churri Sauce (recipe, page 280).

## Wine Notes

Pinot noir again is the choice, but this preparation adds a deeper smoke quality to the fish. Therefore, a richer pinot noir is required. The Sonoma Coast and Green Valley appellations in California produce wines that show rich berry fruit and firm but elegant tannins. Look for offerings from Flowers and Lynmar. ■

# Smoked Salmon Dip with Parmesan-Roasted Asparagus

## Wine Notes

*While pinot noir is the*

*natural choice for salmon,*

*the Parmesan and asparagus*

*are too powerful for this*

*delicate red. A rich, robust*

*white from the Rhône is*

*much better suited. A crozes*

*hermitage blanc from Remezier*

*with its bold and aromatic*

*nose, clean acidity and delicate*

*fruit is a worthy choice.* ■

---

1/2 POUND SLICED, COLD-SMOKED SALMON
4 OUNCES CREAM CHEESE, ROOM TEMPERATURE
1/2 CUP SOUR CREAM
1 TABLESPOON CHOPPED DILL
KOSHER SALT AND GROUND BLACK PEPPER
1 POUND ASPARAGUS
1/4 CUP EXTRA VIRGIN OLIVE OIL
3 TABLESPOONS PARMESAN CHEESE
1 LOAF FRENCH BREAD

1. Place the sliced smoked salmon in the bowl of a food processor and process until smooth. Add the cream cheese and pulse to combine. Add the sour cream and dill and combine. Season with salt and black pepper. Transfer the salmon dip to a decorative bowl.

2. Preheat the oven to 350 degrees.

3. Remove the tough white lower sections from the asparagus spears. Peel the lower two to three inches of tough outer skin from the bottom of the asparagus. Place the asparagus on an ovenproof pan and drizzle with olive oil. Sprinkle with salt, pepper and the Parmesan cheese. Bake in a preheated oven for 15 minutes.

4. To serve, slice the French bread into 1/2-inch slices. Cut the asparagus spears in half crosswise and serve on the side with the salmon dip.

# Whole Lemon and Garlic-Smoked Chicken

1 ROASTING CHICKEN (ABOUT 4 TO 4 1/2 POUNDS)
1 LEMON
8 WHOLE GARLIC CLOVES, PEELED
10 WHOLE BLACK PEPPERCORNS

1. For this recipe, the chicken is soaked or brined in a mixture of water and salt. Rinse the chicken and remove any excess fat or skin. Place the chicken in a large pot and cover with brine (¾ cup kosher salt and 1 gallon cold water). Place the pot in the refrigerator and allow the chicken to brine for about 1½ hours for every pound of chicken weight (e.g., a 4-pound chicken should soak in the brine for 6 hours).

2. Remove the chicken from the brine and pat dry with paper towels. Halve the lemon and place in the cavity of the chicken along with the peeled garlic cloves and whole peppercorns. Truss the chicken by tying the legs together for a more uniform shape.

3. Hot smoke the chicken at 350 degrees, breast side up, for 40 minutes using about 2 Tablespoons hickory chips. A large item such as this chicken will require you to "tent" the smoker with aluminum foil because the lid will not close.

4. After the chicken is smoked, place it in a preheated 350-degree oven to roast for about 45 minutes or until the internal temperature of the thigh registers 170 degrees.

## Wine Notes

*The succulent, smoky flavors of the meat and the lemony garlic are the perfect foil for the elegant acidity and citrusy fruit of Californian fume blanc. Grgich Cellars in Napa Valley produces a wine of impressive character that would not only add to this dish, but would serve well with a salad or as an aperitif.* ■

# SMOKING SEAFOOD—SCALLOPS, SHRIMP, TROUT AND MUSSELS

SMALLER FOODS require a fine mesh rack to support them. I use a small cooling rack that fits inside the smoker and has a fine square grate. Hot smoke these types of seafood at 350 degrees with 2 Tablespoons mild cherry chips and use the spice rub of your choice, or just salt and pepper for a more neutral flavor.

SCALLOPS: Remove the side muscle from the sea scallops and season with kosher salt and ground white pepper. Smoke for about 15 minutes (depending on the size of scallop) or until firm.

SHRIMP: Remove the shells and veins from large (16–20 count) shrimp and season with kosher salt and ground white pepper. Smoke for about 15 minutes.

TROUT: Place boneless trout fillets skin side down on a lightly oiled rack. Squeeze a little fresh lemon juice over each trout fillet and season with kosher salt and ground white pepper. Smoke for 12 to 15 minutes.

MUSSELS: Clean and de-beard the mussels. Place hinge side down on the smoking rack and smoke for 12 to 15 minutes or until the shells are open and the mussels are cooked through.

## Wine Notes

*Gruner veltliner is Austria's signature grape, and in its simplest form it makes for a light quaffing white. In recent years, higher quality versions have reached our shores and its lovely hints of freesia and cracked pepper spice quality make this wine the perfect match for a variety of smoked fish.* ■

## Wine Notes

*Malbec has long been blended into some of Bordeaux's great wines. But it is in Argentina that it has found its true calling. Deep blackberry fruit is combined with white pepper spice to make the perfect pairing for this tender cut of meat and flavorful sauce. ■*

# GRILL-SMOKED HANGER STEAK WITH A CHIMI CHURRI SAUCE

HANGER STEAK is a very flavorful and tender cut of beef and is very reasonably priced. Rub the steak with Rosemary Steak Rub (recipe, page 283) and hot smoke at 350 degrees with hickory or mesquite chips for about 15 minutes. I like to finish my hanger steak on a hot grill (or grill pan) to sear the outside with a little charred texture and flavor. Serve the hanger steak with Chimi Churri Sauce (recipe follows) and smashed potatoes. I also like to top this dish with crispy fried onion rings.

## CHIMI CHURRI SAUCE

1 TABLESPOON MINCED GARLIC
1½ CUPS VIDALIA ONION, CHOPPED
1 CUP CHOPPED CILANTRO
1 CUP CHOPPED PARSLEY
4 GREEN ONIONS, CHOPPED
2 LIMES, JUICED
1 LEMON, JUICED
1 TABLESPOON KOSHER SALT
2 TEASPOONS GROUND BLACK PEPPER
1½ CUPS EXTRA VIRGIN OLIVE OIL

1. Combine all of the ingredients, except the olive oil, in a food processor and blend until well pureed.

2. With the food processor still running, drizzle in the olive oil until it is well combined.

## ROSEMARY STEAK RUB

1 CUP KOSHER SALT
1/2 CUP DRIED ROSEMARY
1/4 CUP GROUND BLACK PEPPER
1/4 CUP GRANULATED GARLIC

I. Mix all of the ingredients together. Use as is to flavor steaks for grilling or grind finely for a more refined and smooth texture.

## SMOKING SAUSAGE, PORK TENDERLOIN, CHICKEN MEAT AND VEGETABLES

SMOKING FOODS imparts great flavor, but the texture from roasting, searing or grilling is lacking. I prefer to finish meats like sausages, pork tenderloin and chicken in a hot grill pan to add that charred texture and flavor. If you don't have a grill pan, simply sear the meat in a hot, small sauté pan. Season the meats with kosher salt and black pepper or a flavorful rub from the Rubs and Sauces list that follows. Hot smoke at 350 degrees.

RAW ITALIAN SAUSAGE (HOT OR MILD): Smoke 15 minutes and finish in a grill pan for 5 minutes.

PORK TENDERLOIN: Smoke 30 minutes and finish in a hot grill pan for 5 minutes.

CHICKEN BREAST: Smoke 20 minutes and finish in a hot grill pan for 5 minutes.

CHICKEN THIGHS: Smoke 15 minutes and finish in a hot grill pan for 5 minutes.

PORTABELLA MUSHROOMS, PLUM TOMATO HALVES AND ½-INCH-THICK ZUCCHINI SLICES: Smoke 10 minutes and finish in a hot grill pan for 1 minute.

*Wine Notes*

*While no one wine will go with all smoked meats or vegetables, it is safe to assume that the wine should be red. In fact, it should be a red with some body and spiciness, which will lead us to either the syrah or zinfandel grape. Look for wines with rich but not jammy fruit and well-defined peppery spice.* ■

# RUBS AND SAUCES

**RUBS:** Meats that are not cured or brined should be rubbed with various spice blends before smoking to add another dimension to their flavor. I feature several spice blends in my cookbook that lend themselves perfectly to the task at hand.

ROSEMARY STEAK RUB: Grind finely in a spice grinder (recipe, page 283).

CARIBBEAN DRY SPICE MIX: Grind finely in a spice grinder (recipe is in my first cookbook, page 169).

CAJUN SPICE MIX: Use as is (recipe, page 252).

CUMIN SPICE MIX: Use as is (recipe, page 128).

FENNEL SPICE MIX: Use as is (recipe, page 59).

**SAUCES:** Sweet, fruity and acidic sauces match very well with smoked foods. Salsas are terrific and barbecue sauces are also a natural for smoked foods.

MANGO-CILANTRO SALSA (recipe is in my first cookbook, page 89)

PINEAPPLE-AVOCADO SALSA (recipe is in my first cookbook, page 179)

SMOKED TOMATO CONFIT (recipe follows)

HOMEMADE BARBECUE SAUCE (recipe follows)

*If you are looking for a good all-purpose dry barbecue rub, here is a real simple combination of all of the required ingredients: ¼ cup mild paprika, 3 teaspoons kosher salt, 1 teaspoon ground white pepper, 1 teaspoon cayenne pepper and 1 teaspoon granulated garlic. I apply this barbecue rub to ribs, chicken and briskets before I hot smoke them. ■*

## SMOKED TOMATO CONFIT

10 PLUM TOMATOES
5 TABLESPOONS EXTRA VIRGIN OLIVE OIL
KOSHER SALT AND CRACKED BLACK PEPPER
1/2 CUP FINELY CHOPPED YELLOW ONION
1 LARGE GARLIC CLOVE, MINCED
8 OUNCES TOMATO SAUCE
1/2 TEASPOON SWEET PAPRIKA
1/2 TEASPOON GRANULATED SUGAR

*Wine Notes*

*The high acidity of the tomatoes is the perfect match for the bright acidity of Italy's sangiovese grape. A simple chianti or rosso di Montalcino will bring out the best qualities of the dish.* ■

1. Core and halve the tomatoes lengthwise. Place them cut side up on a baking sheet lined with parchment paper and drizzle them with 2 Tablespoons of the olive oil and sprinkle them with kosher salt and black pepper.

2. Smoke the tomatoes for 20 minutes with a fruit wood (cherry or apple) at 200 degrees. If you don't have a smoker, roast the tomatoes in a preheated 375-degree oven for 1 hour. A smoked flavor can be achieved by adding a dash of Liquid Smoke, which is available at most supermarkets.

3. Heat the remaining 3 Tablespoons of olive oil in a medium sauté pan and sweat the onions for 2 minutes over medium-high heat, stirring. Add the garlic and cook briefly. Reduce the heat to medium and add the smoked tomatoes, tomato sauce, paprika and sugar. Cook the mixture over medium heat for 35 minutes or until the mixture becomes very thick.

4. Place the tomato mixture in a food processor and blend to a fine paste. Serve at room temperature.

## HOMEMADE BARBECUE SAUCE

1/4 CUP CANOLA OIL
1 CUP CHOPPED YELLOW ONIONS
2 CLOVES GARLIC, MINCED
2 CUPS DISTILLED WHITE VINEGAR
1/2 CUP BOTTLED CHILI SAUCE
1 CUP TOMATO SAUCE
1 CAN (14 OUNCES) WHOLE TOMATOES WITH JUICE
1 GRANNY SMITH APPLE, PEELED, CORED AND GRATED
3 TABLESPOONS DARK MOLASSES
3 TABLESPOONS DIJON MUSTARD
1 TABLESPOON PAPRIKA
1 TABLESPOON CHILI POWDER
2 TEASPOONS CELERY SEED
1 TEASPOON TABASCO SAUCE
KOSHER SALT AND CAYENNE PEPPER TO TASTE

1. Heat oil in a large saucepan over medium-high heat. Add onions and cook for 2 minutes. Add garlic and cook for 1 minute. Add remaining ingredients and bring to a boil. Reduce to a slow simmer and cook for 90 minutes, stirring occasionally.

2. Puree sauce in a blender until smooth. The sauce will mellow and develop deeper character after a day or two.

*H*

There are millions of barbecue sauce recipes out there and they all have their own individual characteristics. Some are sweet and some are tangy, while others are tomato-based or vinegar-based. Many of these variations can be categorized by region. The western side of the U.S. specializes in tomato-based barbecue sauce while the southern states typically make a vinegar-based version. My sauce is similar to those made in Kansas City, which are thick, tomato-based sauces with molasses. ■

# Annual Maine Lobster Festival

THE ANNUAL MAINE LOBSTER FESTIVAL began in August 1947, in Camden, as a one-day event, where, for $1.00, people could eat all the lobster they wanted as long as the eating took place in one sitting. A big hometown parade marched down Main Street, a submarine chaser control ship moored in Camden Harbor for the festivities, and a street dance provided evening entertainment. More than 10,000 people attended, and a total of 11,960 pounds of lobster was served, a tally that may have been higher if the festival hadn't run out of lobster. It was a sensational success.

One thing is for certain — the Maine Lobster Festival has become an event that attracts people from around the world. It now takes place at Harbor Park in Rockland, during the early days of August, and the celebrating lasts for five days. In addition to all kinds of fresh seafood and all kinds of Maine summer festival food and a pancake breakfast that is served the last four days, lobster remains the focus and is cooked in the world's largest outdoor steamer by many willing volunteers. Though you can no longer eat as much as you want for a $1.00, an incredible amount of lobster is served each year. During the 2005 Maine Lobster Festival, for example, over 25,000 pounds was consumed.

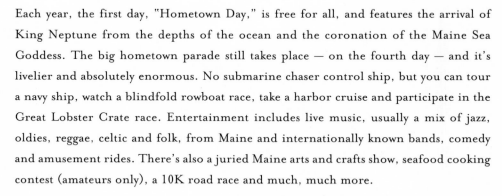

Each year, the first day, "Hometown Day," is free for all, and features the arrival of King Neptune from the depths of the ocean and the coronation of the Maine Sea Goddess. The big hometown parade still takes place — on the fourth day — and it's livelier and absolutely enormous. No submarine chaser control ship, but you can tour a navy ship, watch a blindfold rowboat race, take a harbor cruise and participate in the Great Lobster Crate race. Entertainment includes live music, usually a mix of jazz, oldies, reggae, celtic and folk, from Maine and internationally known bands, comedy and amusement rides. There's also a juried Maine arts and crafts show, seafood cooking contest (amateurs only), a 10K road race and much, much more.

If you love Maine lobster, hanging out in the salt air and thoroughly enjoying yourself, the Maine Lobster Festival in early August is the place to be. ■

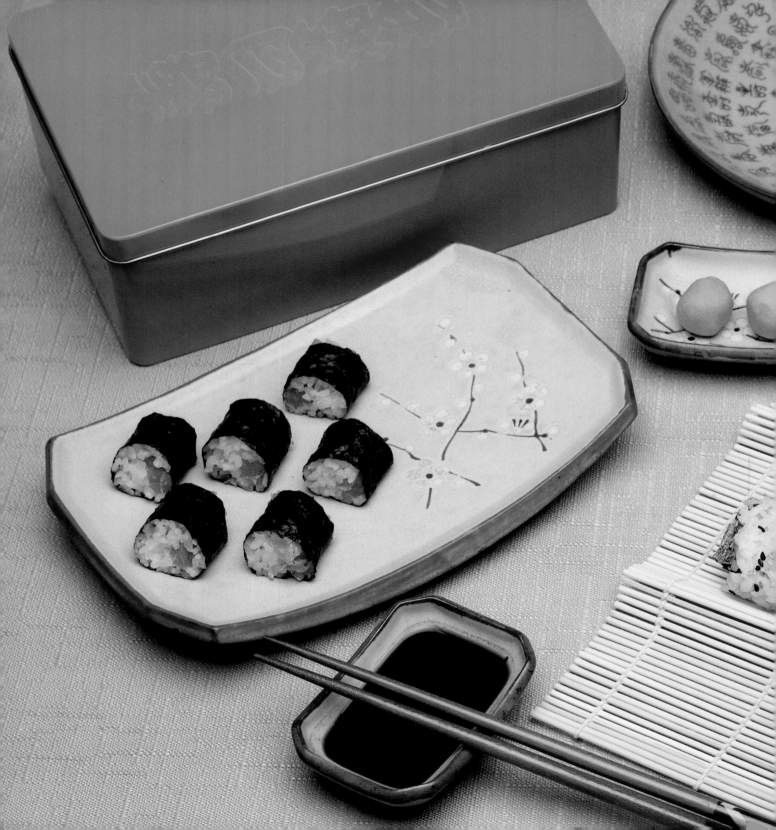

Sushi

$\mathcal{W}$ITH THE POPULARITY OF SUSHI AND JAPANESE CUISINE here in the U.S., it is surprising how few people have attempted to make it for themselves. One of the obstacles that stood in the way was the procurement of specialty products used to make sushi, but the internet has solved this issue with mail-order grocery stores that ship overnight. The other obstacle is technique, which we will try to remedy in this introductory course to making sushi. Over the years in the hotel business, I have made thousands of pieces of sushi for large banquets and specialty functions, and held numerous classes on making sushi. I would like to clarify, however, that I am not a trained sushi chef.

People often confuse sushi with sashimi. The term sushi actually refers to the seasoned rice, whereas the term sashimi means raw fish and is served as simply as that. Sushi is often served with raw seafood but there are many varieties available to those who prefer their food cooked, and when you are rolling your own sushi at home, you can break all the rules and prepare it any way you like. Sushi can be divided into two distinct groups: Maki-Sushi (rolled sushi), like California rolls, and Nigiri-Sushi (finger sushi), where seasoned rice is topped with seafood.

# $\mathcal{S}$HARI (SEASONED SUSHI RICE)

MAKES 10 CUPS RICE

## STEAMED RICE

4 CUPS SHORT-GRAIN WHITE RICE
4 CUPS WATER

1. Place the rice in a large strainer and submerge it in a bowl of cold water to clean it. Remove any impurities and drain the rice. Repeat several times until the water washes away clear.

## Sake Notes

*Sake is the natural*

*accompaniment for sushi,*

*but in many ways it is more*

*confusing than wine. Sake is*

*basically brewed, like a beer*

*would be, but it is considered*

*a rice wine. The flavors can*

*range from incredibly dry and*

*tart to almost sweet, but all are*

*meant to enhance the flavors of*

*the dish that it is served with.*

*While hot sake is better known*

2. If you have a rice cooker, place the rice and water inside and cook for 15 to 20 minutes, following the directions of the manufacturer.

3. To cook on the stovetop, place the rice and water in a small saucepan over low heat and cook covered for 15 minutes.

4. Let the rice rest for 10 minutes before making the shari.

## SHARI ZU (SUSHI VINEGAR)

> 1 CUP JAPANESE RICE VINEGAR
> 1/2 CUP, PLUS 1 TABLESPOON GRANULATED SUGAR
> 2 TABLESPOONS KOSHER SALT
> 1-INCH SQUARE KONBU (KELP)

1. Place the vinegar, sugar and salt in a small saucepan and bring to a boil.

2. Reduce the heat to a simmer and cook for 5 minutes to dissolve the sugar and salt.

3. Remove from the heat and add the kelp square. Cool and store covered in the refrigerator.

## SHARI (SEASONED SUSHI RICE)

> 3 CUPS HOT COOKED RICE
> 1/2 CUP SHARI ZU (SUSHI VINEGAR) (RECIPE ABOVE)

1. Sushi rice is typically stirred in a wooden rice tub or "hangiri" and is gently stirred using a rice paddle. A wooden bowl and spoon will work fine if you don't have these specialized tools.

2. Place the hot rice in the tub and top with the sushi vinegar. Gently and quickly stir the rice in a cutting motion, coating all of the rice with the vinegar. Do not over-stir or the rice will get mushy.

3. Smooth the rice in the tub and let it rest for 10 minutes. Flip the rice over in the tub to distribute any unmixed vinegar and let the rice rest until it is cool. Store in an airtight container to keep it moist. Kept airtight in the refrigerator, and the seasoned (preserved) rice will keep up to a month.

## OTHER BASIC INGREDIENTS AND CONDIMENTS

FURIKAKE: A rice seasoning (many different combinations are available) that is generally made with sesame seeds, nori, dried fish and salt

MAMENORI: Colorful soybean wrappers used as you would nori

NORI: Dried seaweed; look for "yaki nori." The shiny side should always be visible and when the specific roll calls for a half sheet, it is always cut lengthwise

GARI: Pickled ginger

PONZU: Citrus soy sauce usually served with sashimi

RICE VINEGAR: Use Japanese if possible

SESAME SEEDS: Black and white are both available and used in sushi. Toast the white sesame seeds to bring out their optimum flavor

SESAME OIL: A fragrant, dark amber-colored oil pressed from toasted sesame seeds

SHOYU: Japanese soy sauce

WASABI: Japanese horseradish that has an extremely strong flavor. The "heat" from wasabi comes from a burning of the sinus cavity rather than the tongue. The thick green paste is made by mixing powdered wasabi with water. It is also available premixed in a tube

FRESH PRODUCE: Avocado, cucumber (English), radish (daikon) sprouts, citrus, scallion, carrot, alfalfa sprouts

SEAFOOD: Crab, tuna, salmon (cured or smoked; never use raw), snapper, yellowtail, shrimp, scallops, eel, roe (flying fish — tobiko, smelt — masago, or salmon — ikura)

*and more popular in this country, it is cold sake that is of the highest quality and broadest in its flavors. The flavors of sake are best experienced rather than described. While wine descriptions will use the flavors of other fruits to give you a sense of the wine, sake is harder to define. Sake, at first taste, may be a little unusual but it is definitely worth a second try.* ■

## BASIC RECIPES

TEZU (HAND VINEGAR): Hand vinegar is a mixture of 1 cup cold water, 2 Tablespoons rice vinegar and 1 teaspoon kosher salt, and is used to wet your hands when handling sushi rice to keep the rice from sticking to your hands.

### MASAGO AIOLI

3 EGG YOLKS
2 TABLESPOONS LEMON JUICE
1 TEASPOON MINCED GARLIC
1 CUP CANOLA OIL
3 TABLESPOONS MASAGO (SMELT ROE)
KOSHER SALT AND WHITE PEPPER TO TASTE

1. Place the egg yolks, lemon juice and garlic in a small mixing bowl and whisk together for a few minutes until frothy. Slowly drizzle in the canola oil while whisking briskly. Gently mix in the masago and season with salt and white pepper.

### SPICY MASAGO AIOLI

1. Add to the above recipe: 1 Tablespoon Sambal and 3 Tablespoons chopped cilantro.

### CRAB MIX

1. Squeeze the liquid out of 8 ounces cooked crabmeat and mix together with 4 Tablespoons mayonnaise. For Spicy Crab Mix, use the spicy masago aioli in place of the mayonnaise.

## Spicy Tuna Mix

> 1/4 POUND SASHIMI-GRADE TUNA
> 3 TABLESPOONS SPICY MASAGO AIOLI (RECIPE, OPPOSITE PAGE)
> 1 TABLESPOON FINELY CHOPPED GREEN ONION
> 1/8 TEASPOON SESAME OIL
> CAYENNE PEPPER TO TASTE

1. Dice the tuna into small 1/4-inch cubes and mix together with the remaining ingredients.

## Unagi Sauce

This is a great sauce to use with seafood (traditionally made of eel, thus its name).

> 2-INCH SQUARE KONBU (KELP)
> 2 TABLESPOONS KATSUOBUSHI (BONITO FLAKES)
> 2 CUPS SAKE
> 1/2 CUP MIRIN
> 1/2 CUP SHOYU
> 1/2 CUP GRANULATED SUGAR

1. Place the kelp and bonito flakes in a medium-sized saucepan with 1 cup of water. Bring just to a boil and strain out the solids. Return the liquid to the pan and add the remaining items. Cook over medium-high heat until reduced to a light syrup consistency, about 30 minutes. Remove from the heat and let cool. It will thicken more as it cools.

*Ginjyo — Ginjyo rice must be polished to 60 percent of its original size. Ginjyo sake generally possesses more finesse than Junmai. It is usually more aromatic and has hints of fruit flavors in the mouth.* ■

*Dai Ginjyo — The rice in Dai Ginjyo must be polished to at least 50 percent of its original size. Dai Ginjyo flavors are both delicate and complex, and the overall impression is of great harmony.* ■

# Maki-Sushi (rolled sushi)

**BAMBOO SUSHI MAT:** The bamboo sushi mat is a key tool in the preparation of most types of rolled sushi and is essential to forming tight and uniform sushi rolls. The sushi mat is an 8-inch square mat made up of thin bamboo sticks, which are held together by rows of fine string. To use the bamboo sushi mat, lay the mat on the work surface in front of you with bamboo strips going horizontally from you. Nori is placed on the mat followed by rice and fillings, leaving a 1-inch border of uncovered nori at the top. Place your fingers on the ingredients, and with your thumbs, gently bring the bottom end of the bamboo mat up and over the ingredients, tucking the nearest end of the nori in to begin a roll. As the roll starts to form, pull back the rolling mat to keep it from getting rolled into the sushi and continue rolling with light pressure to keep the roll firm and uniform. As you reach the end, lightly wet the exposed border of nori to help seal the sushi and complete the roll.

Maki-sushi, or rolled sushi, can be divided into five classifications, which are differentiated by the way they are rolled and their size:

TEMAKI [Hand Roll]: Temaki are the most informal type of sushi and are called hand rolls because they are simply rolled in your hand by using a half sheet of nori. Temaki come in two basic shapes:

a. Conical: for holding small items like roe, spicy tuna mix or crab mix
b. Cylindrical: for holding larger food items like slices of tuna and sliced vegetables

HOSOMAKI: These are long, thin rolls usually containing one or maybe two fillings. Rolls are made with a bamboo sushi mat by using a half sheet of nori and rolling lengthwise to create a roll that is about 1 inch in diameter. Cut into 6 pieces.

TATEMAKI: These are short, fat rolls with multiple fillings. Rolls are made with a bamboo sushi mat by using a half sheet of nori and rolling widthwise to create a roll that is fat and short. Cut into 6 pieces.

FUTOMAKI [Big Roll]: Rolls are made with a bamboo sushi mat by using a whole sheet of nori and as many toppings as you like. Cut into 8 pieces.

URAMAKI: These are inside out rolls, where the rice is on the outside and the nori is in the center. These can be rolled thin like a hosomaki or fat like a tatemaki. Cut into 6 pieces.

## BASIC ROLLING TECHNIQUE

TEMAKI: Place a half sheet of nori in your hand smooth side down. Wet your hand slightly with hand vinegar and place a "golf ball"-sized ball of sushi rice on the nori paper, spreading it out on the bottom third of the sheet. Top the rice with a little wasabi or aioli, sesame seeds and some of the toppings. Depending on the filling, roll either into a cylinder or cone shape.

HOSOMAKI: Place a half sheet of nori on the bottom edge of a bamboo mat with the long edge of the nori facing you. Spread about 1 cup of sushi rice all over the nori, leaving a ½-inch border along the top. Spread wasabi or aioli in a line down the center of the rice, then sesame seeds and follow with the desired toppings. Use your fingers to hold the toppings in place while your thumbs roll up the bamboo mat. Cover the filling with the bottom edge of the nori, and continue to roll, keeping the cylinder tight and removing the bamboo mat as you go. Tuck in the ends to tidy up the roll and keep the seam of the roll facing down.

TATEMAKI: Follow the same technique as above, changing the orientation of the nori so that the short side is facing the front of the bamboo mat and leave a full 1-inch border on the top without rice to make it easier to close.

FUTOMAKI: Follow the same technique, using a whole sheet of nori and 2 cups of sushi rice. Because it is a larger roll, leave a full 1-inch border on the top without rice.

URAMAKI: Lay a half sheet of nori on the cutting board and spread ½ cup of sushi rice over the entire surface of the nori. Sprinkle the rice with sesame seeds, furikake, masago or finely sliced green onions and flip the rice over, so that the nori is now facing up. Choose whether you would like a thin roll (hosomaki-style) with the long side to the front, or a fat, short roll (tatemaki-style) with the short side to the front. Arrange the spreads and fillings evenly along the bottom third of the nori. Gently roll up the nori and rice in the same manner as above (only without the bamboo mat) using your fingers to keep the filling in place and your thumbs to keep it rolling. Roll into a tight cylinder with the seam down. Top with a small piece of plastic wrap and cover with the bamboo mat. Gently press on the bamboo mat to shape into a squarish cylinder. Tuck in the ends. Remove the bamboo mat and plastic wrap.

## MAKI-SUSHI FILLINGS

Rolled sushi can be filled with anything you fancy, from traditional seafood and vegetables to not so traditional items such as duck and pork. Following is a short list of some of the most popular maki-sushi combinations:

CALIFORNIA ROLL: Crab, avocado and cucumber (futomaki or uramaki)

CALIFORNIA ROLL SPECIAL: Same as above (uramaki) with masago and sesame seeds on outside

CRAB AND ASPARAGUS ROLL: Crab and asparagus (uramaki) with sesame seeds on outside

SPIDER ROLL: Named for its appearance because spider legs come out of the top. Deep-fried soft shell crab, masago aioli, cucumber, pickled ginger and daikon sprouts (futomaki)

PHILADELPHIA ROLL: Smoked salmon, cucumber and cream cheese (futomaki)

SPICY SHRIMP ROLL: Shrimp, avocado, cucumber, spicy masago aioli (uramaki) with masago and sesame seeds on outside

TEMPURA SHRIMP ROLL SPECIAL: Tempura shrimp, avocado, cucumber, cream cheese, masago and Thai sweet chili sauce (futomaki)

TUNA ROLL: Tuna and wasabi (hosomaki)

SPICY TUNA ROLL: Tuna, avocado, cucumber, spicy masago aioli (uramaki) with masago and sesame seeds on outside

RAINBOW ROLL: Crab and cucumber (uramaki) with masago on the outside. Finished with the following items layered on top in colorful rows: tuna, avocado and salmon

## NIGIRI-SUSHI (FINGER SUSHI)

Now that we have gone over the making of maki-sushi, it's time to discuss nigiri-sushi. Nigiri-sushi is very simple in concept, but quite a bit more difficult in proper execution. Traditionally, oblong rice balls are made by hand and topped with seafood, usually raw fish or shellfish, with a little wasabi smeared on it. The topping should cover the top of the rice. If the topping does not form well to the top of the rice (like with tamago — omelet) then a strip of nori (1 inch by 4 inches) is wrapped around the topping and rice to secure it. Nigiri-sushi is served in pairs.

## FLASH-FRIED NORI AND TUNA ROLL WITH A GINGER-WASABI BUTTER SAUCE

SERVES 2

1/4 POUND SASHIMI-GRADE TUNA
1 SHEET OF NORI, CUT IN HALF LENGTHWISE
1 CUP FRESH ARUGULA
1/2 CUP CILANTRO LEAVES
1/4 TEASPOON FURIKAKE
DASH OF SHICHIMI
CANOLA OIL FOR FRYING

*These Flash-Fried Nori and Tuna Rolls are out of this world with their crisp Panko-tempura exterior and soft tender interior of fresh tuna. Yum! Experiment with other fillings too. The Ginger-Wasabi Butter Sauce is a great match for this dish, with its French origins and Japanese flavors. The creaminess of the sauce balances with the heat of the wasabi and perfectly complements the crispy roll.* ■

*Yamahai Shikomi* — Similar
to the Kimoto method, but in
place of the labor-intensive
work of breaking up the rice and
aerating with poles, lactic acid is
used to stabilize the brew. ▪

*Namazake* — Namazake
is a fresh, aromatic sake,
analogous to draft beer.
Typically, Namazake is
pasteurized only once rather
than once after fermentation
is completed and again at
bottling. ▪

ALL-PURPOSE FLOUR
TEMPURA BATTER (RECIPE FOLLOWS)
PANKO BREAD CRUMBS
GINGER-WASABI BUTTER SAUCE (RECIPE FOLLOWS)
SESAME SEEDS, SLICED SCALLIONS AND CILANTRO
SPRIGS FOR GARNISH

1. Cut the tuna into 1-inch strips.

2. Lay the nori sheets, shiny side down and long side to you. Spread the arugula and cilantro leaves over the entire nori sheet, leaving a small border on the top to seal the roll.

3. Divide the tuna strips between the two sheets, laying them across the center. Sprinkle the tuna with the furikake and the shichimi.

4. Tightly roll the tuna inside of the nori and wet the top border of the nori with a little hand vinegar to seal it tight. Repeat with the other roll.

5. Heat the canola oil in a small deep-fat fryer or heavy saucepan (3 inches of oil) to 350 degrees. Roll the tuna rolls in flour, to evenly coat, dip them into the tempura batter, lightly drain off excess and roll in the Panko bread crumbs, to evenly cover. Gently place the battered rolls into the hot fryer and cook, turning frequently, for about 2½ to 3 minutes. The rolls should be golden brown, but you only want to cook the very outside of the tuna, leaving the inside bright red.

6. Set the rolls on a paper towel to drain briefly, slice each roll into 6 equal pieces and lay them on a bed of the ginger-wasabi butter sauce. Sprinkle with sesame seeds and scallions. Garnish with cilantro sprigs and serve immediately.

## GINGER-WASABI BUTTER SAUCE

1/3 CUP UNSALTED BUTTER
1 TABLESPOON CANOLA OIL
2 TABLESPOONS CHOPPED YELLOW ONION
1/2 CUP WHITE WINE
1 TABLESPOON PEELED AND MINCED FRESH GINGER
1/2 CUP HEAVY CREAM
1 TABLESPOON LIME JUICE
2 TABLESPOONS SWEET CHILI SAUCE
2 TEASPOONS WASABI PASTE
2 TEASPOONS COARSELY CHOPPED FRESH CILANTRO
2 TABLESPOONS SOY SAUCE (SHOYU)

1. Dice the butter and bring to room temperature.

2. Heat the oil in a small 2-quart saucepan. Sauté the onions over medium heat for 2 minutes but do not allow them to brown. Deglaze with the white wine, add the ginger and reduce over medium heat until most of the liquid has evaporated. Again, do not brown. Add the heavy cream and reduce the mixture by half, whisking occasionally.

3. Remove the pan from the heat and immediately whisk in the butter until well incorporated. Strain through a fine mesh strainer into a small bowl, discarding the solids. In a small bowl, combine and mix together the lime juice, sweet chili sauce, wasabi paste, cilantro and soy sauce. Stir this mixture into the butter sauce and keep in a warm place (not too hot or it will break) until serving.

*Nigori — The word means cloudy. Nigori receives a rough filtering leaving fine particles of rice and Koji from the fermentation. The resulting sake has a complex aroma and plenty of flavor. Before modern filtration, all sake was Nigori. ∎*

*Taruzake — Taruzake is sake that has been aged in Cypress barrels. The wood imparts a spicy, woody flavor that is a pleasant complement to sake. ∎*

1/2 CUP RICE FLOUR
1/2 CUP ALL-PURPOSE FLOUR
1 TEASPOON KOSHER SALT
1 1/2 TO 2 CUPS CLUB SODA

1. Mix the flours and the salt together in a mixing bowl and whisk in enough of the club soda to make a batter the consistency of pancake batter.

# CRAB AND PAPAYA ROLL WITH A SWEET CHILI PEANUT SAUCE

### SERVES 4

2 SHEETS MAMENORI (SOYBEAN WRAPPERS),
    COLOR OF YOUR CHOICE
3 CUPS MESCLUN (BABY MIXED GREENS)
1 POUND CRAB MIX (RECIPE, PAGE 296)
1 POUND FRESH PAPAYA, PEELED, SEEDED AND
    CUT INTO 1-INCH STRIPS
1/4 ENGLISH CUCUMBER, THINLY SLICED
1/4 CUP DRY-ROASTED PEANUTS, LIGHTLY CRUSHED
1/2 CUP CILANTRO LEAVES
A LITTLE SUSHI RICE TO USE AS GLUE
SWEET CHILI PEANUT SAUCE (RECIPE FOLLOWS)

1. Mamenori sheets are more fragile than regular nori, so use a little more care when rolling. Lay the full mamenori sheets out on bamboo mats.

2. All of the ingredients will be divided evenly between the two sheets of mamenori. Lay the mesclun on the mamenori, covering the bottom 2/3 of the sheets. Place a row of crabmeat down the center of the mesclun reaching the

---

*Mamenori is an edible soybean paper that can be used in place of nori paper when rolling sushi. It comes in a rainbow of colors (yellow, orange, green or pink), which creates a beautiful presentation when wrapped around spring rolls or used in rolling sushi. Mamenori is great for those who dislike the flavor of nori paper allowing them to enjoy sushi without the seaweed flavor. Rarely available in retail markets, your best bet is to purchase mamenori online. ∎*

entire length of the sheet. Set the papaya strips next to the crab, cover with the cucumber slices, a sprinkling of crushed peanuts and cilantro.

3. Place a small row of sushi rice along the top of the mamenori sheet (this will act as glue to hold the roll together) and gently roll it, pressing firmly with the bamboo mat and seal it with the rice.

4. Slice each roll into 4 equal pieces and serve with the sweet chili peanut sauce.

## SWEET CHILI PEANUT SAUCE

> ½ CUP SWEET CHILI SAUCE
> 1 TEASPOON COARSELY CHOPPED FRESH CILANTRO
> 1 TABLESPOON COARSELY CHOPPED ROASTED PEANUTS
>     (UNSALTED)
> 1 TABLESPOON RICE WINE VINEGAR

1. Combine all the ingredients and mix well. *Keep the sauce covered in the refrigerator, for up to 1 week.*

# GLOSSARY: JAPANESE SUSHI TERMS

ANAGO: Saltwater eel

EBI: Shrimp

FURIKAKE: Rice seasoning made of sesame seeds, nori, dried fish and salt

FUTOMAKI: Big sushi roll

GARI: Pickled ginger

GOMA: Sesame seeds: Kuro Goma (black sesame seeds); Shiro Goma (white sesame seeds)

HAMACHI: Young yellowtail (variety of tuna)

HANGIRI: Rice tub

HOSOMAKI: Long, thin sushi rolls

IKURA: Salmon roe

KAIWARE: Daikon sprouts

KANI: Crabmeat

KOMBU: Kelp

MAGURO: Tuna: the most commonly used are yellowfin, bigeye and bluefin

MAKI SU: Bamboo mat

MAKI-SUSHI: Rolled sushi

MAMENORI: Soybean wrap, which comes in a variety of bright colors

MASAGO: Smelt roe, which is also known as "Capelin roe"

MIRIN: Sweet rice wine

NEGI: Green onion

NIGIRI: Oblong rice ball topped with seafood, usually raw fish or shellfish, and served in pairs

NIGIRI MOLD: Plastic or wooden mold used to form oblong rice balls for nigiri

NIGIRI-SUSHI: Finger sushi

NORI: Dried seaweed

OSHINKO: Pickled vegetables

PANKO: Japanese bread crumbs, which are light, crispy and coarser than regular bread crumbs

PONZU: Citrus soy sauce

SABA: Mackerel

SAKE: A drink (rice wine) and salmon: slightly different pronunciation for each

SAMBAL: Or sambal oelek is a hot pepper sauce used as a condiment in Indonesia

SHAMOJI: Rice paddle

SHARI: Seasoned sushi rice

SHARI ZU: Sushi vinegar

SHICHIMI: Seven spice pepper

SHOYU: Japanese soy sauce

TAI: Sea bream, which is a type of fish not readily available in the U.S.; use snapper

TAMAGO: Rectangular egg omelet

TATEMAKI: Short, fat sushi rolls

TEMAKI: Hand roll, informal sushi rolled in your hand, most common form is cone-shaped

TOBIKO: Flying fish roe

UNAGI: Freshwater eel

URAMAKI: Inside out sushi roll

WAKAME: Seaweed used in miso soup and the famous Goma Wakame or sesame seaweed salad

YUZU: Japanese citrus fruit; if you can't find it, use lemon juice

# Camden Hiking

WITHIN MINUTES OF DOWNTOWN CAMDEN, scores of interesting and varied trails exist for your hiking pleasure. They range in degree of difficulty, and round-trips can take as little as twenty minutes and as long as five hours.

Camden Hills State Park, not even two miles north of downtown Camden, offers over 30 miles of well-marked and groomed trails on its 5,700 acres. Choosing among the different trails can be a challenge. If you love open vistas, four mountaintop trails you might want to try are Maiden Cliff, Adam's Lookout, Megunticook and Mt. Battie. Once you reach the summit of Maiden Cliff, you'll be standing 800 feet above beautiful Megunticook Lake and will have spectacular 360° views of the lake and the Georges Highlands. Adam's Lookout, with an elevation of 1,180 feet, gives you stunning views of Penobscot Bay and its many charming islands. Megunticook, a moderately easy trail, pays off with incredible views of the ocean, lakes and hills. And, the Mt. Battie Trail, both a moderate and strenuous hike, opens to the summit of Mt. Battie, which provides breathtaking views of the bay, several of its islands, Camden Harbor and the village of Camden itself. If you prefer lowland hiking, the Sky Blue Trail offers three hours of tranquility as you move through mature forests and blueberry barrens. Or, there's Shoreline Trail that winds along the rugged coastline of Penobscot Bay. These are all great places for a picnic and for keeping an eye out for bald eagles, ospreys, turkey vultures and red-tailed hawks, especially during fall hawk migration. You can choose among 20 different trails, and they are open year-round during daylight hours.

The Georges Highland Path, also open year-round during daylight hours, offers over 35 miles of hiking all the way from Thomaston and Rockland to Rockport and Camden to Searsmont and Montville. The Bald Rock Mountain/Ragged Mountain section of the Georges Highland Path is minutes from downtown Camden. These summits rise over 1,200 feet and offer spectacular views of the Georges River watershed all the way to Maine's western hills and beyond to Mount Washington and the White Mountains of New Hampshire. The Ragged Mountain recreational area is located less than two miles west of Camden while Bald Rock Mountain is just minutes northwest of Camden. Should you decide to hike the seven miles between them that includes

both summits, you are in for a spectacular hike that is steep and strenuous in places and immensely popular.

Both the Camden Hills State Park and the Georges Highland Path provide some of the most outstanding coastal mountain hiking in all of New England, so don't forget to pack your hiking boots. ∎

# INDEX

*H*